Skyline 1

Resource Pack

Susan Banman Sileci

Ana Maria Cuder

MACMILLAN

Introduction

The *Skyline* Resource Pack contains thirty-six communicative activities for beginner students of English. It is designed to be used with *Skyline* Student's Book 1 but can be used to supplement any course.

The activities can be used for extension and consolidation purposes after target language is introduced, or be used later in the course as revision.

Teachers often ask about how to use resource packs. Here are some of the most frequently asked questions, together with answers.

Should I review target language with the class before students begin the activity?

There are different schools of thought. Some teachers argue that by not reviewing the language they have a better idea of which students can activate the language and which students need further help. Other teachers prefer to review the target language briefly in the hope that students will use it throughout the activity. There is no reason why a teacher cannot experiment with both approaches. If you decide to preview the target language, it is better to make it very brief, two to five minutes is usually enough. It may help less confident students to have a model of the target language on the board to refer to if they need it.

How do I teach students the rules for a game?

It's easier, and clearer to the students, if you show them how to play a game rather than explain the rules at length. One way is to model or show how the game works. Choose a student from the class to demonstrate the activity with you. It may not always be necessary to model the whole activity.

Students often want to speak in their mother tongue. How can I stop them?

Students speak in their mother tongue for a number of reasons. First they may not understand why they are doing an activity so it is helpful to explain the purpose and the final aim of an activity at the beginning. Second students may not understand what to do. Demonstrating the activity should resolve this problem by showing them what is expected of them. Finally students may also lack confidence or feel they do not have enough English to do the job properly. Modeling the task before the activity starts will enable students to be clear about the type of language they might use. Encouragement, as in everything, is also a very important motivational force.

What should I correct and when should I correct it?

This will depend on the aim of each activity. In general, it is helpful to limit areas of correction to the main aim of each activity. It may be that other areas of correction arise out of an activity. Many teachers find it helpful to note errors down under different categories while they are monitoring. Possible categories could be: target language, pronunciation or appropriacy of language use.

It is generally more productive not to stop students during an activity unless there is a breakdown in communication. Feedback can then take place directly after the activity or at a later point. It is important that students are given feedback on two areas: task performance and language performance.

Can I use these activities if my classes are very large or very small?

Yes, you can. If your class is large, try dividing it in half or in thirds. Each group then carries out the activity at the same time while you walk around and monitor the class. In this case, it's especially important to model the activity and make sure that students understand the procedures. If your class is small, some activities may need to be modified. For example, eliminate some cards or alter the rules to suit the circumstances.

What can I do to discourage students from looking at each other's worksheets or cue cards?

Most of the activities in the pack are based on the principle of an 'information gap' – that is, student A knows something that student B does not know, and vice versa. It's useful to explain this to students from the beginning of the course and tell them that when they look at each other's cue cards or worksheets it destroys the need to exchange information.

Students may also look at each other's information because they lack confidence in their English. It is helpful to stress that struggling to form questions or correct answers is a natural and useful part of the language learning process.

A further reason why students look at each other's material is because they aren't clear about how to do an activity. Careful demonstrating of an activity and constant encouragement should help. If there is enough space, students could sit face to face, or back to back.

Some students work more quickly than others. How can I handle this?

This situation is inevitable. Setting and keeping the time limits suggested in the activities can help, although your students may need more or less time. If the activity has two or more parts, make sure that a time limit is set for each part. If you find that some students always finish the activity before the set time limit, be prepared with an extra activity for them. Often the corresponding optional activity or additional activity in the Resource Packs can be used in these situations.

My students always seem to choose the same partners for pair work activities. Is this a good idea?

People tend to sit with people they like regardless of the type of class they are in but from a teacher's point of view it is better if students change partners. Sometimes it's helpful to explain the benefits of working with different people. For example, it improves rapport in the classroom and adds an element of interest and surprise to question and answer sequences. Students may then understand why they should change partners.

If your class is small, you could try keeping a small envelope with the names of every student on a piece of paper. Pull out two pieces of paper at a time and get these two students to be pairs for a particular activity. With larger classes, you can divide the class into two groups. Students on the the left side of the room will be students A in a pair work activity and the students on the right side will be students B. The left side then mixes with the right side and partners can be chosen accordingly. The next time, divide the class in half by front and back so students can't predict where you'll divide the room.

Should I monitor the activity if students are familiar with the grammar and know how the activity works?

Yes, most definitely. Monitoring is a very flexible teaching technique. Initially, many students feel nervous about having a teacher listen to them, but once that has disappeared they usually appreciate the attention. Monitoring offers you the chance to walk around the classroom and informally evaluate how well students are doing. You can give specific language input and encouragement to individuals and groups. It makes it easier to tackle the inevitable problem of students using their own language in the class too. At the same time it allows you to build a working relationship with individuals and smaller groups, which is something that is more difficult to do with larger classes. If you carry a pen and paper you can also note recurring problems for review at the next opportunity.

What do I do if there's an odd number of students in the class for pair work activities?

You can ask the extra student to model the activity with you for the rest of the class. Another possibility is to ask the extra student to work with a pair of students and either monitor that pair or take turns participating in the activity with them. Remember to rotate students if there's often an odd number so that the same student isn't the "extra" every time. It is not a good idea to participate in the activity yourself to make an even number of students, as this means that you are not free to walk around the classroom and monitor the activity.

It's expensive to make new photocopies every time. How can I save on this expense?

Some activities in the Resource Packs require students to use individual worksheets to answer questions about themselves or their partners. It's best to give fresh copies for this type of activity but, if necessary, you can ask students to write their answers on a separate piece of paper and collect the worksheets for re-use at another time. In some activities, where each student has a worksheet, you could write the information on the board and have students copy it into their notebooks before starting the activity. This way no photocopies are required.

There are many activities which require cutting cue cards or making game boards. For these activities, the same copies can be used over and over if you paste the cue cards or game boards to pieces of cardboard and store them carefully after the activity. Store each activity's copies in a separate envelope or plastic bag and write any necessary information on the outside of the envelope: name of activity, number of copies, number of players necessary or type of activity. Before using the same cards again, check that all the parts are still there so you don't start the activity with your class and only then find missing pairs or copies.

Contents

Worksheet	Interaction	Aim	Time	Skills	Grammar and functions	Vocabulary
1A Questions and answers	Group work	To practice asking and answering questions.	10–15	Speaking Listening	Yes / no questions with the verb to be Information questions Introductions, greetings, personal information	Numbers The alphabet Cities Countries
1B The name game	Group work	To practice using the alphabet.	15–20	Speaking Listening	Spelling names Information questions	The alphabet
1C Mathematical dominoes	Group work	To review numbers 1–20 and the alphabet.	10–15	Speaking	Review of numbers Review of letters	Numbers 1–20 Basic mathematical equations The alphabet
2A Swapping information	Pair work	To practice asking and answering questions using the present simple of to be, third person singular.	10–15	Speaking Listening	Personal information Spelling first / last names Information questions	The alphabet Numbers Nationalities
2B Geography race	Group work	To practice asking and answering questions about countries, capitals and locations.	10–15	Speaking Listening	Information questions Present simple of to be	Countries Continents Capitals
2C Find your partners	Whole class	To practice asking and answering questions about names, cities and countries.	10–15	Speaking Listening	Greetings, introductions Asking and answering questions about personal information Yes / no and information questions	Cities Countries
3A Bingo	Whole class	To review the numbers 1–100.	15–20	Listening	Names of math signs Present simple of to be	Numbers 1–100 Names of math signs
3B Getting to know your classmates	Whole class	To practice asking and answering questions in the present simple.	15–20	Speaking Listening	Yes / no questions with the present simple	Verbs Cognates Likes and dislikes
3C Package tours	Pair work	To practice asking and answering questions with the present simple.	15–20	Speaking Listening Reading	Information questions with the present simple Yes / no questions with the present simple	Travel Nature
4A Perfect love	Whole class	To practice asking and answering questions about personal appearance and preferences.	15–20	Speaking	Asking and answering questions about zodiac signs, birth dates, physical descriptions, likes / dislikes	Signs of the zodiac Hair description Leisure activities and sports
4B Family tree	Group work	To review the vocabulary associated with families.	10–15	Speaking Listening	Asking and answering questions about family members Use of 's to show possession Present simple	Family members
4C Twenty questions	Pair work	To practice and review questions and answers, using the present simple.	15	Speaking Listening	Asking and answering questions about famous people Yes / no questions	Review of words in units 1–4
5A Spot the difference	Pair work	To practice asking and answering questions with is there / are there, there is / there are.	10–15	Speaking	Asking and answering questions about rooms and furniture in a house There is / there are	Rooms Furniture
5B Trivia quiz	Team work	To practice asking and answering questions with the present simple.	10–15	Speaking	Asking and answering questions Review of functions and structures learned in previous units	Numbers & Dates Colors Holidays & Countries
5C What's wrong?	Pair work	To write affirmative and negative sentences with there is / there are + a, an, some, any.	10–15	Speaking Writing	There is / there are + a, an, some, any	The alphabet Months & the zodiac Parts of the body Furniture
6A Guess who?	Whole class	To practice asking and answering questions about daily routine, likes, dislikes and abilities.	15–20	Speaking Listening	Adverbs of frequency Asking and answering questions about daily routine, likes, dislikes and abilities	Sports Leisure-time activities Daily routine Days of the week
6B Job interview	Whole class	To practice asking and answering questions about qualifications and abilities.	15–20	Speaking	can / can't Asking and answering questions about qualifications and abilities	Review of words in unit 6

6C	I'm the President of the United States!	Group work	To practice using the present simple with adverbs of frequency.	15–20	Speaking Listening	Adverbs of frequency Present simple Describing habits, interests and routines	Action verbs
7A	What are they doing?	Pair work	To practice asking and answering questions using the present progressive	15–20	Speaking Listening	Questions and answers using the present progressive Describing and comparing different activities	Action verbs
7B	Are you jealous?	Group work	To practice describing feelings and sharing opinions.	15–20	Speaking Listening	Present simple and present progressive Describing feelings	Adjectives to describe feelings
7C	What word is it?	Team work	To practice defining words.	15–20	Speaking Listening	Recycling present simple and present progressive verbs Defining words	Review of words in units 1–7
8A	Is there a bank?	Pair work	To practice asking and answering questions about places. To practice reading a map.	10–15	Speaking Listening	Asking and answering questions about places *There is / there are* Prepositions of place	Places around town
8B	Cooperative crossword	Pair work	To practice defining and describing places in the city	15–20	Speaking Listening	Defining places around town	Places around town
8C	They're getting married!	Team work	To practice reading and understanding a sequence of events.	15–20	Reading	The present progressive to express plans for the near future	Wedding vocabulary
9A	Mixed recipes	Group work	To practice reading skills.	15–20	Reading Speaking	Imperatives	Foods Words related to cooking
9B	Food race	Pair work	To recycle vocabulary learned in unit 9.	10–15	Speaking	Review of the present simple Information and *yes / no* questions	Different kinds of food Food categories
9C	Health quiz	Group work	To practice talking about food, diets and lifestyles.	15–20	Reading Speaking	Frequency words Information questions with the present simple	Food Eating habits Leisure-time activities
10A	Question line up	Whole class	To practice the present simple and past simple.	15–20	Speaking Listening	Review of major functions learned in previous units Present simple and past simple in information and *yes / no* questions	Review of words from units 1–10
10B	Jumbled biographies	Group work	To use the past simple to reconstruct biographies of famous musicians.	15–20	Reading Speaking Listening	Past simple Connectives	Language used in biographies
10C	What do you know about Diana?	Pair work	To practice asking and answering questions using the past simple	15–20	Speaking	Asking and answering questions about personal information Past simple in information questions	Words related to personal data
11A	How much do you know?	Group work	To review the use of the past simple	10–15	Reading Speaking	Past simple of regular and irregular verbs Discussion of historical and cultural events	Famous people
11B	Once upon a time …	Whole class	To practice describing a sequence of events in the past.	15–20	Speaking Listening	Past simple Connectives	Review of words from units 1–11
11C	What did you have for dinner? last night	Group work	To practice using the past simple in *yes / no* questions and information questions.	15–20	Speaking Reading Listening	Past simple	Review of words from units 1–11
12A	What's Jennifer going to do?	Pair work	To practice using the future with *going to.*	10–15	Speaking Listening	Future with *going to* Talking about future arrangements and plans	Days of the week Clock times Action verbs
12B	What should I do?	Whole class	To practice using the modal auxiliary *should*	15–20	Speaking Reading	Modal auxiliary *should* Describing a problem Asking for and giving advice	Review of words from unit 12
12C	Life's big moments	Whole class	To recycle the present simple, past simple and future with *going to*. To review the modal auxiliary *should*	20–25	Reading Writing Speaking	Present simple Past simple Future with *going to* Giving opinions and justifying them *Should*	Life events Experiences Plans

Questions and answers

Interaction
Group work

Aim
To practice asking and answering questions.

Time
10–15 minutes

Skills
Speaking
Listening

Grammar and functions
Yes / no questions with the verb *to be*
Information questions
Introductions, greetings, personal information

Vocabulary
Numbers
The alphabet
Cities
Countries

Preparation
Photocopy, cut apart and shuffle the question and answer cards. Make sure you have one complete set for each group of five students.

Answers

The questions and answers are in the correct order on the worksheet.

Procedure

1   Divide the class into groups of five.

2   Have each group choose a leader.

3   Give one set of cards to the leader of each group. Ask the leaders to shuffle the cards and give them out to the students in their groups (four cards per student).

4   Explain how to play the game. The goal is to match questions and answers. The first student reads out one of his / her cards aloud. If a student from the group has a matching question or answer, they read it aloud. Matching pairs of questions and answers should be placed on the table in the middle of the group. Students continue asking and answering in turn until they have completed all the matches.

5   The first group to finish the activity correctly wins. Ask the rest of the groups to finish matching their pairs also.

Option
This could also be a whole class activity. Prepare enough question cards for half the class and the matching answer cards for the other half. If you have an odd number of students, ask two students to work together as one. Give a card to each student. Ask students to walk around the class, reading their questions or answers to their classmates until they find their partners.

Additional ideas
Make enough photocopies of the whole page for half the students. Cut the pages in half vertically, making two separate sets – one set with questions and one with answers. Distribute them randomly to the class. Students with questions write answers for them and those with answers make up suitable questions.

Questions and answers

Questions   NAME?   **Answers**   YES

?

Questions	Answers
What's your name?	My name is Sandra.
Where are you from?	I'm from France.
How do you spell your first name?	M-I-C-H-A-E-L.
How do you spell your last name?	J-O-N-E-S.
How are you?	I'm fine, thanks.
Are you a good student?	Yes, I am.
Are you from New York?	No, I'm not. I'm from Los Angeles.
Is Julie a producer?	Yes, she is.
What's your telephone number?	It's 234-9847.
What's this [backpack] in English?	It's a backpack.

YES   NO   ?

NUMBER?   COUNTRY?   CITY?

Skyline Resource Pack 1. Published by Macmillan Publishers Limited.

The name game

Interaction
Group work

Aim
To practice using the alphabet.

Time
15–20 minutes

Skills
Speaking
Listening

Grammar and functions
Spelling names
Information questions

Vocabulary
The alphabet

Preparation
Photocopy and cut apart name cards. Make sure you have one card for each student in the class.

Answers

The names are in alphabetical order (from left to right) on the worksheet.

Procedure

1 Write these two questions on the board: *What's your first name? How do you spell it?* Ask students to form pairs and ask each other these questions.

2 Then ask the whole class to put themselves in alphabetical order of first names. Tell them to speak only in English as they do this. Check that the order is correct.

3 Now divide the students into two, three or four groups.

4 Explain that they are going to play a similar game but that they won't use their real names. Give each student a name card and ask them to memorize their new name.

5 Explain how to play the game. Students from the same group take turns spelling their names and lining up in alphabetical order. Encourage them not to look at their cards as they do this.

6 The first group to do the activity correctly wins. Check by asking individual students to spell their new names.

7 If time allows, the groups can then work together to put all the students in the class in alphabetical order, forming one line.

Option
Divide the students into two teams, A and B, and give each student a name card. Have each team choose a leader and ask the leaders to stand at the board. In turn, students from each team spell their names and the leader from the other team writes them on the board. Encourage students not to look at their cards but don't be strict about this. When they have finished, check that the names are written correctly. The group with the most correct names wins.

Additional ideas
Shuffle the cards and give them out, one to each student. Ask students to move around the room and find someone whose name has the same initial letter as theirs. (Not every student will find a partner.) Set a time limit of five minutes.

The name game

Agamemnon	*Aristotle*	**Billy Bob**	***Bronwyn***	Cosmo
Cuthbert	Deidra	**Euripedes**	**Ezekiel**	**Floramaria**
Garfield	Giuseppe	*Hedwig*	Humperdink	Ignatius
Josephina	Kaikura	Kathi Lee	Llewellyn	**Maximilian**
Mordecai	Nuncio	Ophelia	Pebbles	Quincy
Quirino	Rocky	*Shaquille*	**Soloman**	Tallulah
Tyrone	Ulysses	Vasilis	Vaughn	Winifred
Wolfgang	Xanthus	*Yorick*	Zachary	**ZENEVIEVA**

Skyline Resource Pack 1. Published by Macmillan Publishers Limited.

Mathematical dominoes

Interaction
Group work

Aim
To review numbers 1–20 and the alphabet.

Time
10–15 minutes

Skills
Speaking

Grammar and functions
Review of numbers
Review of letters

Vocabulary
Numbers 1–20
Basic mathematical equations
The alphabet

Preparation
Photocopy and cut apart one set of dominoes for each student.

Procedure

1 On the blackboard, review the mathematical signs: $+$, $-$, $\div$, x.

2 Divide the class into groups of four and give each student a set of dominoes.

3 Explain the game to the students:

- Each group shuffles all the dominoes and places them face down on the table in front of them.

- Each student takes four dominoes.

- Player A puts down any domino face up, at the same time correctly saying the letter on the domino or correctly solving the equation.

- Player B must then put a domino next to player A's domino which matches one of its sides, e.g. *an equation with another equation*. Player B must also say the letter or solve the equation on the domino they lay down.

- The players take turns playing dominoes in this way.

- If a player can't put down a domino, he / she takes one from the center of the table.

- The first player to use all his / her dominoes wins.

Additional ideas
If time allows, students can make up their own dominoes to add to the game, basing them on the information learned in *Skyline* units 1 and 2. They can include names of countries or question and answer pairs, e.g.
What's your name? / My name is Suzanna.
Where are you from? / I'm from Brazil.
Remind them that each domino must have a corresponding pair so that the game can be played properly.

Mathematical dominoes

14 − 3 =	7 x 2 =	K	A
E	G	9 + 5 =	U
10 + 10 =	U	I	G
9 − 6 =	8 + 9 + 2 =	J	5 x 4 =
K	15 − 11 =	20 − 9 =	J
20 ÷ 5 =	I	18 ÷ 6 =	17 + 2 =
K	Q	E	Q

Swapping information

Interaction
Pair work

Aim
To practice asking and answering questions, using the present simple of *to be*, third person singular.

Time
10–15 minutes

Skills
Speaking
Listening

Grammar and functions
Personal information
Spelling first / last names
Information questions

Vocabulary
The alphabet
Numbers
Nationalities

Preparation
Photocopy the worksheet, one for each pair of students. Cut each page in half between the Student A and Student B sections.

Answers

First name: Helmut
Last name: Schroeder
Nationality: German
Telephone number: 657-896-7105
Class: Intermediate

First name: Akemi
Last name: Yamanaka
Nationality: Japanese
Telephone number: 212-754-0643
Class: Elementary

Procedure

1 Divide the students into two groups, A and B.

2 Give the students in the A group the student A sections and those in the B group the student B sections. Allow them a few minutes to read the instructions.

3 Play the role of a student A and model the task with a student B, as follows:
   Teacher: *What's Helmut's last name?*
   Student B: *It's Schroeder.*
   Teacher: *(writing on board) Schroeder? How do you spell that?*
   Student B: *S-C-H-R-O-E-D-E-R.*

4 When students understand the activity, ask them to form A / B pairs and begin asking and answering. Tell them not to look at each other's cards.

5 When the students have completed the activity, ask them to compare their cards to check the information they have each written.

Option
After the students have completed the activity and compared their cards, have them write a short paragraph about each character.

Additional ideas
For extra practice in spelling names and saying telephone numbers, tell the students to imagine they have lost their address books. Have them move around the class, asking their classmates for their names and telephone numbers and writing the information down on a piece of paper. Allow them five minutes to do this. When the time is up, check how many names and addresses the students have collected. The student with the most wins.

Swapping information

Student A

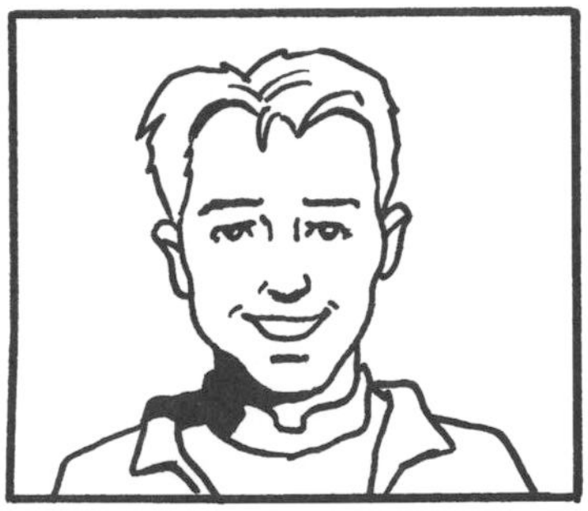

First name: Helmut

Last name:

Nationality: German

Telephone number:

Class: Intermediate

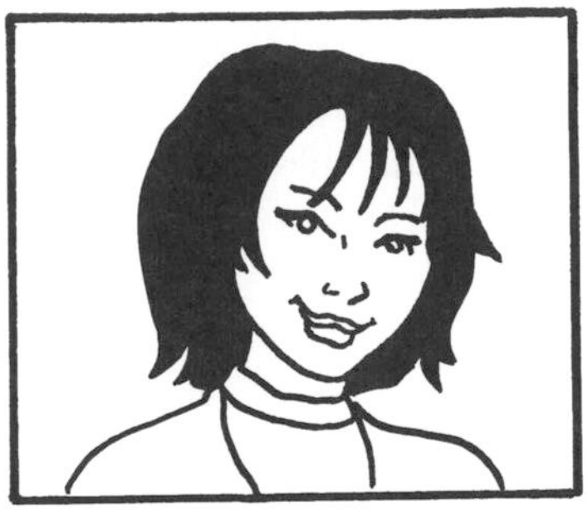

First name:

Last name: Yamanaka

Nationality:

Telephone number: 212-754-0643

Class:

Student B

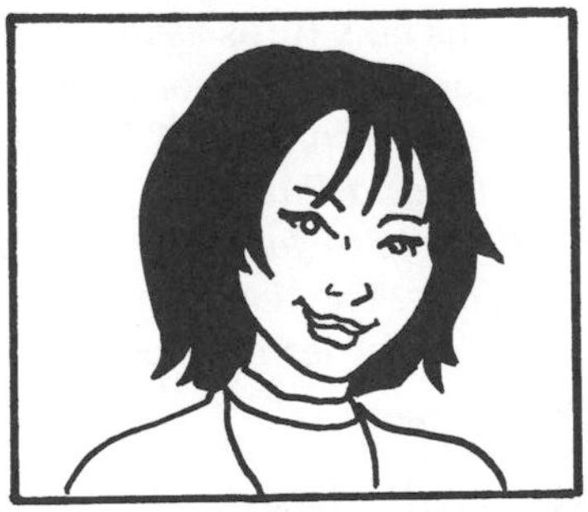

First name: Akemi

Last name:

Nationality: Japanese

Telephone number:

Class: Elementary

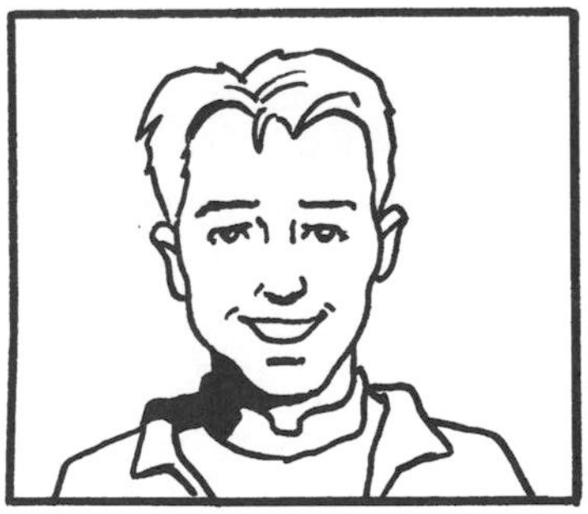

First name:

Last name: Schroeder

Nationality:

Telephone number: 657-896-7105

Class:

Skyline Resource Pack 1. Published by Macmillan Publishers Limited.

Geography race

Interaction
Group work

Aim
To practice asking and answering questions about countries, capitals and locations.

Time
10–15 minutes

Skills
Speaking
Listening

Grammar and functions
Information questions
Present simple of *to be*

Vocabulary
Countries
Continents
Capitals

Preparation
Photocopy the worksheet and cut apart the cards. Make sure you have a complete set for every five students.

Answers
The answers are in the correct order on the worksheet.

Procedure
1 Divide the class into groups of five.
2 Explain the game. Each group receives 32 different cards. These cards are distributed to the members of each group but held secret until the signal to begin is given. Groups race to put their cards into correct groups of four, made up of a country, its capital, neighboring countries and continent. The first group to put all their cards into the correct groups wins.
3 Write a few sample questions on the board before the game starts, for students to model, e.g. *Is Saudi Arabia in the Middle-East? Are Namibia and Zambia neighbors of Angola? What's the capital of Hungary?*
4 Give the signal to begin the game.
5 When a group has won, check its answers and ask the rest of the groups to finish.

Option
The cards can be used to play a quiz game. Divide the students into two teams, A and B. Give each team the sets of cards for four of the countries. Each team chooses a spokesperson. The spokespersons take turns asking the other team three questions about one of their countries, e.g. *What's the capital of India? What continent is it on? China and Pakistan are India's neighbors – true or false?* Each correct answer is worth one point. The team with the most points when all the countries have been asked about is the winner.

Additional ideas
Students can choose one country on the list and write a simple paragraph about it. Encourage them to use an atlas or an English encyclopedia to add a few details.

Geography race

Country: India	Country: Guyana
Capital: New Delhi	Capital: Georgetown
Location: Asia	Location: South America
Neighbors: China, Pakistan, Nepal, Bangladesh	Neighbors: Venezuela, Brazil, Suriname
Country: Ireland	Country: Saudi Arabia
Capital: Dublin	Capital: Riyadh
Location: Europe	Location: Middle-East
Neighbors: Wales, England, Scotland	Neighbors: Kuwait, Iraq, United Arab Emirates, Qatar
Country: Angola	Country: Hungary
Capital: Luanda	Capital: Budapest
Location: Africa	Location: East Central Europe
Neighbors: Namibia, Zambia, Congo-Kinshasa	Neighbors: Slovakia, Austria, Yugoslavia, Romania
Country: Canada	Country: Laos
Capital: Ottawa	Capital: Vientiane
Location: North America	Location: Southeast Asia
Neighbors: The United States	Neighbors: China, Vietnam, Cambodia, Thailand

Find your partners

Interaction
Whole class

Aim
To practice asking and answering questions about names, cities and countries.

Time
10–15 minutes

Skills
Speaking
Listening

Grammar and functions
Greetings, introductions
Asking and answering questions about personal information
Yes / no questions
Information questions

Vocabulary
Cities
Countries

Preparation
Before class, photocopy and cut apart the cards. Make sure you have enough matching pairs for the number of students. If you have an odd number of students, ask two students to work together as one.

Answers

Italy: Dario Panucci and Roberta Di Donni
Germany: Heinrich Rüger and Claudia Matthes
Australia: Tim Watkins and Marcia Collins
Romania: Paula Armanar and Nicolae Penes
Morocco: Fatimah El Geurrouj and Hicham Khannouchi
USA: Mike Edwards and Stephanie Logan
France: Jean-Pierre Michelot and Laura Arnat
Colombia: Juan Pablo Rodriguez and Miranda Espada
Brazil: Gustavo Franco and Fernanda Mierelles
Korea: Su Chon Choi and Kye Sun Hi
Mexico: Marta Martinez and Raul Hernandez
Japan: Yuko Seko and Tadahiro Emoto

Procedure

1   Review the structures necessary for this activity by choosing a student and eliciting basic personal information about him / her. Ask questions like *What's your name? What city are you from? Are you from Costa Rica?* Write this information on the board.

2   Now ask this student to elicit the same information from another student. Write the questions on the board if he / she has difficulty asking correctly.

3   When you are satisfied that the class is comfortable with the basic questions to ask, begin the activity.

4   Shuffle the cards and give one card to each student. Ask them to read and memorize their imaginary names and cities / countries of origin.

5   Set the scene: they are at an international conference and they are taking part in the opening-night cocktail party.

6   Ask students to move around the class, introduce themselves to other students and talk about where they are from. When they find someone who is from the same country as themselves, have them sit down.

7   Finish the activity when the time is up or when all the students have found their partners.

8   As a follow-up, students could be asked to introduce their new friend to the class, e.g. *This is my friend Laura. She's French. She's from Toulouse.*

Option
Students can play a memory game with the cards. Make one copy of the worksheet for each pair of students and cut the cards apart. Students put them face down on the table and take turns turning two cards over. If the countries on the cards match, the student keeps the cards. If not, they put them face down again. They continue until all the pairs have been found. The student with the most pairs wins.

Find your partners

Name:	Dario Panucci
City:	Milan
Country:	Italy

Name:	Stephanie Logan
City:	Cleveland
Country:	USA

Name:	Heinrich Rüger
City:	Hamburg
Country:	Germany

Name:	Miranda Espada
City:	Bogotá
Country:	Colombia

Name:	Tim Watkins
City:	Sydney
Country:	Australia

Name:	Raul Hernandez
City:	Mexico City
Country:	Mexico

Name:	Paula Armanar
City:	Craiova
Country:	Romania

Name:	Tadahiro Emoto
City:	Tokyo
Country:	Japan

Name:	Fatimah El Guerrouj
City:	Marrakech
Country:	Morocco

Name:	Claudia Matthes
City:	Frankfurt
Country:	Germany

Name:	Mike Edwards
City:	Kansas City
Country:	USA

Name:	Marcia Collins
City:	Melbourne
Country:	Australia

Name:	Jean-Pierre Michelot
City:	Paris
Country:	France

Name:	Kye Sun Hi
City:	Seoul
Country:	South Korea

Name:	Juan Pablo Rodriguez
City:	Buenaventura
Country:	Colombia

Name:	Marta Martinez
City:	Mérida
Country:	Mexico

Name:	Gustavo Franco
City:	Fortaleza
Country:	Brazil

Name:	Yuko Seko
City:	Osaka
Country:	Japan

Name:	Su Chon Choi
City:	Ulsan
Country:	South Korea

Name:	Fernanda Mierelles
City:	São Paulo
Country:	Brazil

Name:	Nicolae Penes
City:	Bucharest
Country:	Romania

Name:	Roberta Di Donni
City:	Rome
Country:	Italy

Name:	Hicham Khannouchi
City:	Casablanca
Country:	Morocco

Name:	Laura Arnat
City:	Toulouse
Country:	France

Unit 3A   *Teacher's Notes*

Bingo

Interaction
Whole class

Aim
To review the numbers 1–100.

Time
15–20 minutes

Skills
Listening

Grammar and functions
Names of math signs
Present simple of *to be*

Vocabulary
Numbers 1–100
Names of math signs

Preparation
Photocopy and cut apart the bingo cards. Make sure you have one for each student.

Masterboard

1	2	3	4	5	6	7	8	9	10
11	12	13	14	15	16	17	18	19	20
21	22	23	24	25	26	27	28	29	30
31	32	33	34	35	36	37	38	39	40
41	42	43	44	45	46	47	48	49	50
51	52	53	54	55	56	57	58	59	60
61	62	63	64	65	66	67	68	69	70
71	72	73	74	75	76	77	78	79	80
81	82	83	84	85	86	87	88	89	90
91	92	93	94	95	96	97	98	99	100

Procedure
1 On the blackboard, review the mathematical signs: +, −, ÷, x.
2 Give each of the students a card and ask them to write a different number from 1–100 in each of the sixteen squares. Remind students not to repeat numbers.
3 Start saying simple math calculations aloud, e.g. *three times three*.
4 Students mentally work out the calculation and check if they have the number nine on their cards. If they do, they cross it out. At the same time, circle or cross out the number nine on your master board (see left).
5 Continue making simple calculations until a student has crossed out all the numbers on his / her board. This student shouts *Bingo* and if his / her numbers are all correct, he / she wins the game.
6 Some sample calculations you can make are, e.g. *19 − 7 (12), 90 ÷ 3 (30), 10 x 4 (40), 20 + 32 (52)*.

Option
Working with numbers 1–100 might take too long. In this case, limit the range of numbers for the game to 1–50 or 51–100. Alternatively, instead of stopping the game after a student has crossed out all the numbers on his card, stop the game after a student has crossed out one complete line of numbers (vertically, horizontally or diagonally).

Additional ideas
Divide the class into two teams. Each team makes up ten simple math calculations involving numbers 1–100. Each team leader reads their team's calculations and the other team gives the answers. A correct answer scores one point. The team with the highest score wins.

Bingo

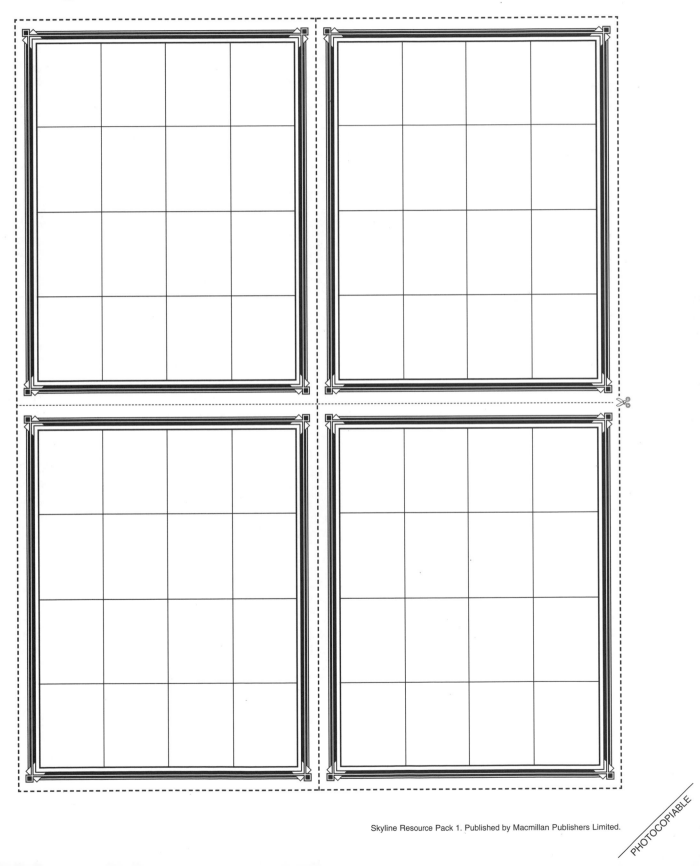

Getting to know your classmates

Interaction
Whole class

Aim
To practice asking and answering questions in the present simple.

Time
15–20 minutes

Skills
Speaking
Listening

Grammar and functions
Yes / no questions with the present simple

Vocabulary
Verbs
Cognates
Likes and dislikes

Preparation
Photocopy and cut apart the question cards, one for each student in the class.

Procedure
1 Give the students a card each. Allow them a minute to read the information and decide on the question they are going to ask their classmates.

2 Ask them to get a pen / pencil and a piece of paper or a notebook for this activity.

3 Explain how to play the game. Students move around the room asking their classmates questions in order to find out how many of them answer *Yes* to their question. When they find someone in the class who does, they write the student's name down on a piece of paper.

4 Model the activity by asking a few students a question like *Do you like Japanese food?* If they answer *Yes*, write their names on the board.

5 Set a time limit of five to eight minutes and ask them to begin the activity.

6 When the time is up, invite individual students to report their results to the class, e.g. *Two students speak Spanish. They are Miguel and Roberta.*

Option
Students can work in pairs to ask and answer these questions with a partner. They make a note of their answers and write a short paragraph about their partner, mentioning several affirmative answers they received and several negative answers, e.g. *My partner doesn't have a pet and he doesn't have a job. He loves Hollywood movies but he doesn't like rap music.*

Additional ideas
Choose a topic on one of the cards and ask questions about it in such a way that students start an interesting class discussion. For example, you might choose *Find out how many students give to charities* and ask students questions, e.g. *What is a charity? Do you give to a charity? Are charities always honest?* Encourage everyone in the class to give ideas and opinions.

Getting to know your classmates

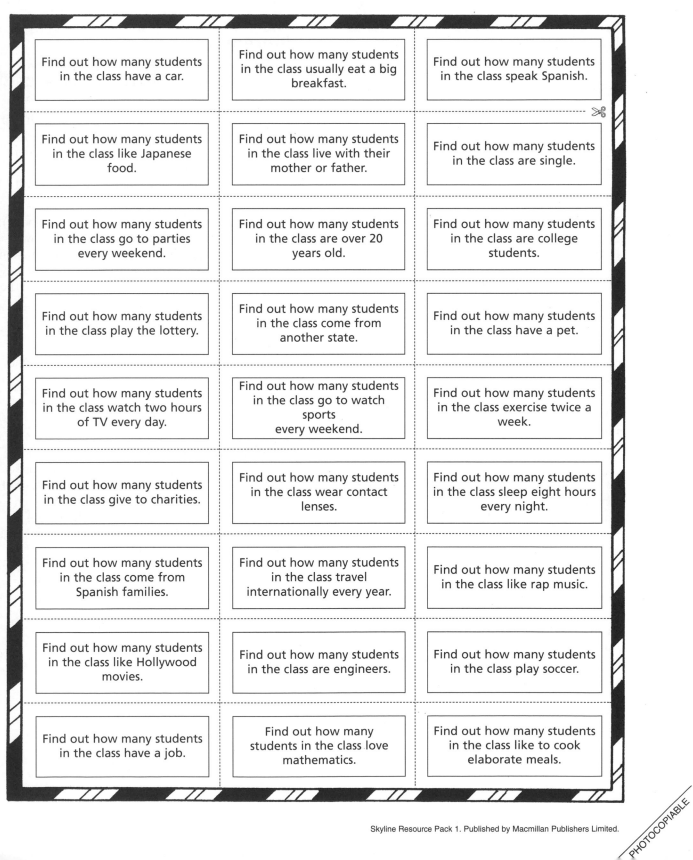

Find out how many students in the class have a car.	Find out how many students in the class usually eat a big breakfast.	Find out how many students in the class speak Spanish.
Find out how many students in the class like Japanese food.	Find out how many students in the class live with their mother or father.	Find out how many students in the class are single.
Find out how many students in the class go to parties every weekend.	Find out how many students in the class are over 20 years old.	Find out how many students in the class are college students.
Find out how many students in the class play the lottery.	Find out how many students in the class come from another state.	Find out how many students in the class have a pet.
Find out how many students in the class watch two hours of TV every day.	Find out how many students in the class go to watch sports every weekend.	Find out how many students in the class exercise twice a week.
Find out how many students in the class give to charities.	Find out how many students in the class wear contact lenses.	Find out how many students in the class sleep eight hours every night.
Find out how many students in the class come from Spanish families.	Find out how many students in the class travel internationally every year.	Find out how many students in the class like rap music.
Find out how many students in the class like Hollywood movies.	Find out how many students in the class are engineers.	Find out how many students in the class play soccer.
Find out how many students in the class have a job.	Find out how many students in the class love mathematics.	Find out how many students in the class like to cook elaborate meals.

Skyline Resource Pack 1. Published by Macmillan Publishers Limited.

Package tours

Interaction
Pair work

Aim
To practice asking and answering questions with the present simple.

Time
15–20 minutes

Skills
Speaking
Listening
Reading

Grammar and functions
Information questions with the present simple
Yes / no questions with the present simple

Vocabulary
Travel
Nature

Preparation
Photocopy and cut apart the A / B cards. Make one set for each pair of students.

Answers

Student A
Name of tour: Mother Earth Adventures
Hotel: None Tour dates: June 12 – June 19
Food: Chilean and American
Places to visit: caves, pools, canyons
Guides: speak Spanish & English
Price: $2,900 – Includes: all meals, tents, rafts
Phone number:1-800-999-5436

Student B
Name of tour: The Amazon Forest!
Hotel: Amazon Inn Tour dates: March 26 – April 1
Food: Local specialties
Places to visit: Rio Negro, canoe trip to see alligators
Guides: speak English, Portuguese, Spanish & German
Price: $1,250 – Includes: Hotel, all meals, tours
Phone Number: 1-800-334-8685

Procedure

1 Ask students what kind of information they would ask for before booking a vacation. Elicit words, e.g. *price, hotel, activities and dates*.

2 Set the scene: One of the students in each pair wants to travel to a certain place and needs information about the tour. The other student will play the role of the travel agent and answer the client's questions. Then they will change roles.

3 Divide the students into two groups (A and B). Hand out the student A / B cards and allow students a few minutes to read the information on their cards. Answer any questions they may have about the vocabulary or structures on the cards.

4 Elicit possible questions they might ask each other and write them on the board.

5 Pretend you are student B and play the game with a student A.

6 Set a time limit of fifteen minutes and ask students to do the activity in A / B pairs.

Additional ideas
Ask students to work individually or in groups to make a mock pamphlet about a tour, e.g. a tour of their neighborhood or a local natural attraction. Alternatively they can do research and create a pamphlet about an international attraction such as the Grand Canyon or a wildlife park in Africa. Students should then present their tours to the rest of the class. Encourage them to keep the writing simple, using the present simple and illustrating their pamphlets with their own drawings or pictures from magazines.

Package tours

Student A

Name of tour: _____

Hotel: _____

Tour dates: _____ Food: _____

_____

Places to visit: _____

Guides: _____

Price: _____

Price includes: _____

Phone number: _____

The Amazon Forest!

Come with Amazon Expeditions to see trees, birds, exotic animals and, of course, native people. The water is fresh, the nights are clear and the river is spectacular. Our next tour begins on March 26 and ends seven days later, on April 1. Our experienced guides are natives of Brazil and Venezuela and speak English, Portuguese, Spanish and German. Tourists stay at the charming Amazon Inn and eat wonderful local seafood specialties such as *tucunaré* and *pirarucú*. Our tours include excursions to the Rio Negro and an alligator-watching journey in a motorized canoe.

Amazon Expeditions cost $1,250 per person. This price includes hotel, three meals a day and all programmed tours. Call now at 1-800-334-8685 to book your trip!

Student B

Name of tour: _____

Hotel: _____

Tour dates: _____ Food: _____

_____

Places to visit: _____

Guides: _____

Price: _____

Price includes: _____

Phone number: _____

Mother Earth Adventures

Rafting in Patagonia ... that's an adventure! You don't want to miss Mother Earth Adventures' next trip down the Futaleufú River from June 12 to June 19. For only $2,900, you can run the rapids, dance with butterflies and see South American nature at its best.

Our guides are the best Chile has to offer, speaking both Spanish and English. We serve excellent food including Chilean specialties and American favorites. Guests sleep in tents or caves – there are no hotels on the trip. We take guests down the river and show them the caves, pools and canyons that only the Futaleufú River offers. Included in the price are all meals, tents and, of course, the rafts. Call us now at 1-800-999-5436 for more information.

Perfect love

Activity
Whole class

Aim
To practice asking and answering questions about personal appearance and preferences.

Time
15–20 minutes

Skills
Speaking

Grammar and functions
Asking and answering questions about zodiac signs, birth dates, physical descriptions, likes / dislikes

Vocabulary
Signs of the zodiac
Hair description
Leisure activities and sports

Preparation
Before class, photocopy and cut apart the A / B cards. Make sure you have enough matching pairs for the number of students. To find the pairs, look at the type of hair described. There are exactly two of each hair style. If you have an odd number of students, ask two students to work together as one.

Procedure

1   Give one card to each student. As far as possible, give the A cards to women and the B cards to men. If necessary, explain that some students will have to role play the opposite sex.

2   Allow students some minutes to read the information on their cards.

3   Tell them that the object of the game is to find their perfect love. To do this they have to move around the class asking questions until they find someone whose tastes match theirs in at least three areas.

4   Remind students that they are not allowed to show their cards to the others in the class.

5   If necessary, elicit the questions they might ask and write them on the board, e.g. *What is your hair like? Are you an Aries? When is your birthday? Do you like doing aerobics?*

6   When the time is up, or as soon as all the students are paired up, check if they have paired up correctly. Ask pairs questions, e.g. *What are the things you have in common? What do you like doing?*

Option
Instead of asking students to walk around the classroom, ask them to work in groups of five. This is especially useful for large classes. Give each student in the group two cards, chosen at random. Without showing their cards to other members of the group, students talk about their cards. The first group to make all ten matches is the winner.

Additional ideas
Ask students to write a paragraph for homework describing their ideal mate. They should write about as many aspects of this ideal person as they can: his / her likes and dislikes, physical attributes, zodiac sign, nationality, etc.

Perfect love

	Group A			Group B
You have: Birthdate: You like:	short black hair March 1 playing basketball running reading		You like:	long brown hair playing baseball watching TV playing soccer Capricorns
You have: Birthdate: You like:	long black hair October 29 watching TV cooking going to movies		You like:	Scorpios going to movies listening to music reading long black hair
You have: Birthdate: You like:	short red hair August 15 seeing friends watching TV cooking		You like:	reading playing basketball running Cancers long red hair
You have: Birthdate: You like:	long red hair June 30 playing baseball reading watching TV		You like:	short gray hair Geminis running cooking playing soccer
You have: Birthdate: You like:	short blond hair September 27 reading playing soccer seeing friends		You like:	going to movies listening to music dancing long blond hair Aquariuses
You have: Birthdate: You like:	long blond hair February 2 dancing playing baseball playing basketball		You like:	Virgos doing aerobics listening to music seeing friends no hair
You have: Birthdate: You like:	short brown hair April 22 listening to music playing soccer running		You like:	short brown hair playing soccer running playing basketball Tauruses
You have: Birthdate: You like:	long brown hair January 6 playing basketball playing baseball seeing friends		You like:	swimming reading playing basketball Pisceses short black hair
You have: Birthdate: You like:	no hair September 10 swimming going to movies doing aerobics		You like:	watching TV doing exercise going to movies Leos short red hair
You have: Birthdate: You like:	short gray hair May 31 running listening to music going to movies		You like:	short blond hair Libras seeing friends playing baseball swimming

Skyline Resource Pack 1. Published by Macmillan Publishers Limited.

Family tree

Interaction
Group work

Aim
To review vocabulary associated with families.

Time
10–15 minutes

Skills
Speaking
Listening

Grammar and functions
Asking and answering questions about family members
Use of 's to show possession
Present simple

Vocabulary
Family members

Preparation
Photocopy one family tree for each group and cut apart the five clues at the bottom.

Answers

1st row: Nancy / Bill (or) Bill / Nancy
2nd row: Beverly / Mark / Carl (or) Mark / Beverly / Carl
3rd row: Greg / Laura (or) Laura / Greg

Procedure

1   Divide the class into groups of five students and give each student an information card and each group a copy of the blank family tree. Alternatively, teachers could give each student in the group a copy of the blank family tree.

2   The groups should sit in circles, if possible. If there are fewer than five students in a certain group, some students might have to work with more than one information card.

3   Explain that each group should use the clues to fill in the family tree. Taking turns, each person in the group reads one of the clues in his / her information card aloud.

4   One person acts as a secretary and is responsible for filling in the blank family tree with the input of the rest of the group.

5   When the time is up or when they've finished, check their answers either orally or by drawing a blank tree on the board and asking different groups to fill it in with you.

Option
Instead of using the worksheet, students can make their own family trees. They can then talk about their family trees with a partner. If time allows, the partner can explain his / her partner's family tree to the rest of the class.

Additional ideas
Ask students to form pairs and interview their partners. Student A should make a family tree for student B and then student B should make a family tree for student A.

Family tree

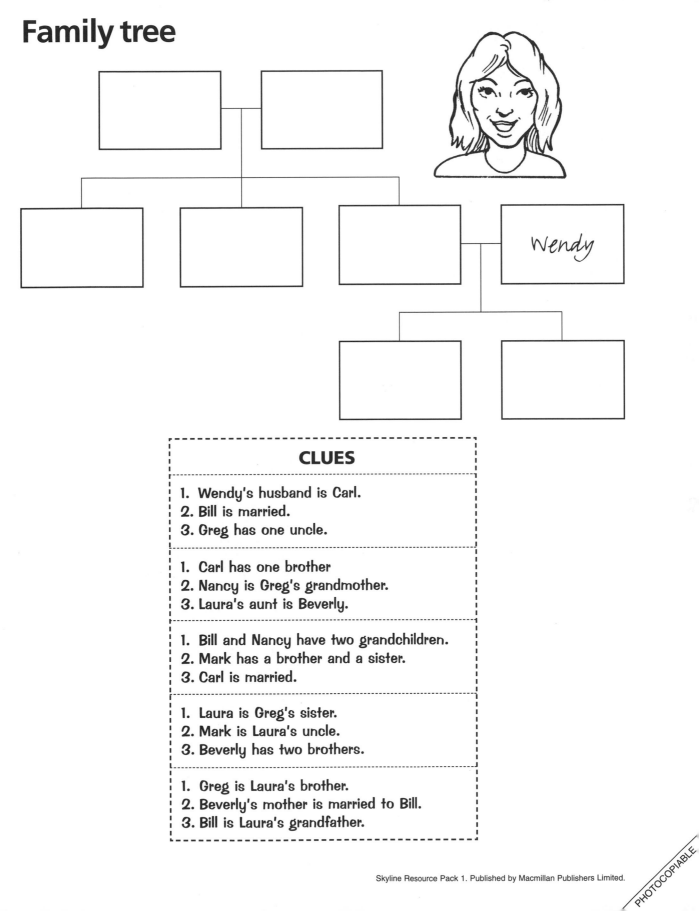

Wendy

CLUES

1. Wendy's husband is Carl.
2. Bill is married.
3. Greg has one uncle.

1. Carl has one brother
2. Nancy is Greg's grandmother.
3. Laura's aunt is Beverly.

1. Bill and Nancy have two grandchildren.
2. Mark has a brother and a sister.
3. Carl is married.

1. Laura is Greg's sister.
2. Mark is Laura's uncle.
3. Beverly has two brothers.

1. Greg is Laura's brother.
2. Beverly's mother is married to Bill.
3. Bill is Laura's grandfather.

Twenty questions

Interaction
Pair work

Aim
To practice and review questions and answers, using the present simple.

Time
15 minutes

Skills
Speaking
Listening

Grammar and functions
Asking and answering questions about famous people
Yes / no questions

Vocabulary
Review of the words learned in units 1–4

Preparation
Photocopy the worksheet. Make one copy for each pair of students in the class.

Procedure

1 Divide the students into pairs.

2 Give one worksheet to each pair and allow them a few minutes to familiarize themselves with the question types.

3 Explain how to play the game. Student A should think of a famous person who is alive and write that name on a piece of paper. Student B should not know who student A has chosen. Student B must ask *yes / no* questions and try to discover the name of the person student A has chosen. Student A can answer only with *yes* or *no* and short answers (*Yes, he is. / No, she doesn't.*)

4 Student B is allowed only 20 questions to discover who student A has chosen. If he / she does not succeed with 20 questions or less, student A wins and can reveal who his / her person is. Student B then thinks of a famous person who is alive and student A asks questions.

Option
This can be played as a group. One student (or you) should think of a famous person who is alive and the class members take turns asking questions. To make sure all students participate, suggest that they ask in order of where they are seated. Students must wait their turn to ask a question, even if they know the answer. The person who guesses correctly gets to think of a famous person for the next round.

Additional ideas
Write the names of famous people (all of them should be well known by the students) on blank white stickers. Place one tag on each student's forehead. Students should move around the room asking questions about themselves (*yes / no* questions only) until they guess who they are.

Twenty questions

politician	singer
actress / actor	athlete
dancer	author

Possible questions:

Is it a man?

Is she American?

Is he an actor?

Does she have a famous husband?

Is she funny?

Is she old?

Is he in famous Hollywood movies?

Does he live in Europe?

Does he make romantic movies?

Does she wear a swimsuit on TV?

Do women think he's handsome?

Does she sing and dance?

Is he tall?

Does he have gray hair?

Is she on TV?

Spot the difference

Interaction
Pair work

Aim
To practice asking and answering questions with *is there / are there, there is / there are.*

Time
10–15 minutes

Skills
Speaking

Grammar and functions
Asking and answering questions about rooms and furniture in a house
There is / there are

Vocabulary
Rooms
Furniture

Preparation
Photocopy the worksheet and cut apart the A / B cards. Make enough copies for each pair of students to have an A card and a B card.

Answers

House 1
There are two beds in the bedroom.
There is no (There isn't a) closet in the bathroom.
There is one window in the kitchen.
There are two cars in the garage.
There are a man, a woman and three children (a family) in the dining room.
There is a dog in the yard, next to the doghouse.
There is a stereo in the living room.

House 2
There is one bed in the bedroom.
There is a small closet in the bathroom.
There are two windows in the kitchen.
There is one car in the garage.
There are a man and a woman in the dining room.
There is a cat in the yard, next to the bush.
There is a TV in the living room.

Procedure
1 Divide the students into two groups, A and B.
2 Give each student in the student A group an A card and each student in the student B group a B card.
3 Explain what students A and B must do. Their cards show a picture of a two-story house. The houses are very similar, but there are six differences between them. They have to find out what the differences are by asking each other questions.
4 Allow them one or two minutes to study their pictures. Answer any questions they might have about vocabulary and question structure.
5 Elicit possible questions they can ask each other and write them on the board, e.g. *How many _____ are there in your house? Is there a / an _____ in the bedroom? Are there any _____ in the kitchen?*
6 If necessary, role model the part of a student A with a student B.
7 Ask students to form A / B pairs and start the activity.
8 After approximately ten minutes, or when students have finished, check answers. Ask individual students to tell the class the differences they have found.

Additional ideas
If time allows after checking students' answers, ask students to write a short paragraph describing their own houses. To help students begin, write some basic guidelines on the board, e.g.
I live in a two-story house with _____.
In my house there's _____, _____, _____ and _____.
I share a bedroom with _____.

Spot the difference

Student A

Student B

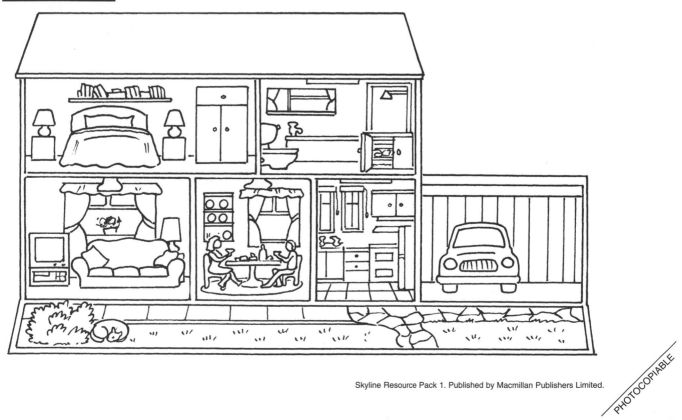

Trivia quiz

Interaction
Team work

Aim
To practice asking and answering questions with the present simple.

Time
10–15 minutes

Skills
Speaking

Grammar and functions
Asking and answering questions
Review of functions and structures learned in previous units

Vocabulary
Numbers
Dates
Colors
Holidays
Countries

Preparation
Photocopy the worksheet and cut apart the A / B cards. Make enough copies for each pair of students to have an A card and a B card.

Procedure
1   Prepare students for the activity by asking different students sample questions, e.g. *How many colors are there in the American flag?* (3 – red, white and blue) Check students' answers with the whole group.

2   Divide the class into two teams, A and B.

3   Give a copy of the team A card to each student on team A and a copy of the team B card to each student on team B.

4   Explain the activity. They are going to test each other's knowledge by asking the questions listed on their cards. Ask members of each team to choose a representative who will be responsible for giving the agreed answer to the other team.

5   Allow students a minute to familiarize themselves with the information on their cards. Answer any questions they might have.

6   Ask one student to keep the score. He / she should give one point for every correct answer.

7   Team A starts by choosing one student to ask team B the first question on their list. When team B has answered, they can choose a student to ask team A the first question on their list. Continue until all questions have been asked.

8   The team with the highest score wins.

Option
Cut out the answers and set them aside. Give the questions to pairs of students. Set a time limit of 10 minutes and have them answer the questions. When the time is up, check the answers. Give one point for every correct answer. The pair / group with the highest score wins the competition.

Additional ideas
Ask students to work in groups and prepare their own trivia quizzes, writing down the questions and answers on separate pieces of paper. Collect their papers and give them out to different groups. Ask each group to answer the questions. Give the answers back to the original group to check.

Trivia quiz

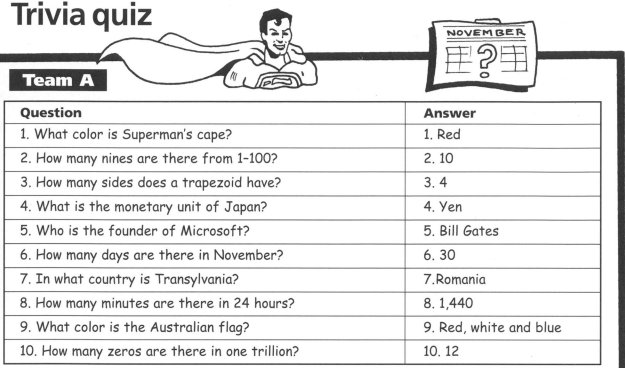

Team A

Question	Answer
1. What color is Superman's cape?	1. Red
2. How many nines are there from 1–100?	2. 10
3. How many sides does a trapezoid have?	3. 4
4. What is the monetary unit of Japan?	4. Yen
5. Who is the founder of Microsoft?	5. Bill Gates
6. How many days are there in November?	6. 30
7. In what country is Transylvania?	7. Romania
8. How many minutes are there in 24 hours?	8. 1,440
9. What color is the Australian flag?	9. Red, white and blue
10. How many zeros are there in one trillion?	10. 12

Team B

Question	Answer
1. How many weeks are there in a year?	1. 52
2. What color is Peter Pan's shirt?	2. Green
3. How many hours are there in two weeks?	3. 336
4. How many states are there in the United States?	4. 50
5. When is Halloween?	5. October 31
6. What is the monetary unit of Germany?	6. Mark
7. What color is the Canadian flag?	7. Red and white
8. Who is the female star of Titanic?	8. Kate Winslet
9. How many colors are there on the McDonald's logo?	9. 3 (red, yellow, white)
10. What's the capital of Indonesia?	10. Jakarta

What's wrong?

Interaction
Pair work

Aim
To write affirmative and negative sentences with *there is / there are + a, an, some, any.*

Time
10–15 minutes

Skills
Speaking
Writing

Grammar and functions
There is / there are + a, an, some, any

Vocabulary
The alphabet
Months
The zodiac
Parts of the body
Furniture

Preparation
Photocopy the worksheet, one for each student.

Answers

1 There aren't any eyes on the man's face. / The eyes are missing. 2 There are five legs on one of the chairs. 3 There is a toilet in the kitchen. 4 There is a snowman on the beach. 5 There are three Pisces in the picture / on the zodiac wheel. 6 There aren't any ears on the rabbit's head. / The ears are missing. 7 There isn't an E and there isn't a K. / The letters E and K are missing. 8 There isn't a last name. / The last name is missing. 9 There isn't a keyboard. / The keyboard is missing. 10 There aren't any windows. / The windows are missing. 11 There is a refrigerator in the bedroom. 12 There are two Januarys on the calendar.

Procedure

1 Prepare students for the activity by drawing an envelope on the board. Write the name of the person and the city, country and zip code, but deliberately omit the address, e.g. *Julia Richardson, Seattle, Washington, 98117, U.S.A.*

2 Ask students to tell you what's wrong with the envelope. Ask questions like: *Is there a name on it? Is there a city?*

3 Give each student a copy of the worksheet and ask them to form pairs.

4 Explain the activity. In pairs, they study the pictures and decide what's wrong with each one. They then write sentences about each picture. Sentences should start with *There is / There are / There isn't / There aren't.*

5 Set a time limit of about ten minutes and ask students to start the activity.

6 When the time is up, check students' answers by asking different pairs for their answers. Does everyone in the class agree? Elicit all possible responses.

Option
Ask students to do the activity in groups of four. The first group to come up with all the correct answers in the shortest amount of time wins.

Additional ideas
Ask each pair to think of one idea which is similar to the worksheet. One by one they should draw their pictures on the board while the other pairs try to guess what's wrong. The student who is drawing on the board can elicit correct answers from the rest of the class.

What's wrong?

Guess who?

Interaction
Whole class

Aim
To practice asking and answering questions about daily routine, likes, dislikes and abilities.

Time
15–20 minutes

Skills
Speaking
Listening

Grammar and functions
Adverbs of frequency
Asking and answering questions about daily routine, likes, dislikes and abilities

Vocabulary
Sports
Leisure-time activities
Daily routine
Days of the week

Preparation
Photocopy the worksheet. Make sure there is one for each student in the class.

Procedure

1 Prepare students for the activity by asking individual students questions like: *What do you usually do on the weekends? What kind of movies do you like?*

2 Give one worksheet to each student.

3 Explain the first part of the activity. Students should complete the sentences with information about themselves. Tell students not to write their names on their sheets.

4 Set a time limit of five minutes for this part of the activity. When time is up, collect the worksheets.

5 Shuffle them and give them out again, one to each student. Be careful not to give a student his / her own worksheet.

6 Allow them one or two minutes to read the information on their sheets.

7 Explain the second part of the activity. They should move around the room, asking their classmates questions until they discover who wrote the information on their worksheet. Emphasize that they should not show their worksheet to anyone else and that the only way to discover who wrote the answers is by asking questions from the worksheet.

8 Elicit possible questions they are going to ask and write them on the board, e.g. *What do you do on the weekends?*

9 Set a time limit of ten minutes and start the activity.

10 Stop the activity when all students have found the owner of the worksheet they were given.

11 Ask individual students to report their worksheet partner's preferences to the class, e.g. *Marcela always takes a shower before she goes to bed.*

Additional ideas
Ask students to write five sentences about their partner, omitting the partner's name. Have them read their sentences aloud. The other students can guess who the person is.

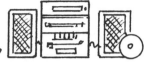

Guess who?

1. I never _____ on the weekend.

2. My favorite sport is _____.

3. I often _____ on Sundays.

4. My favorite movie is _____.

5. I can _____ very well.

6. My favorite day of the week is _____ because

_____.

7. I usually _____ before I go to bed.

8. I can't _____ very well.

9. My favorite song is _____.

10. I love _____!

11. My favorite leisure-time activity is _____

_____.

12. On Sundays, I usually _____.

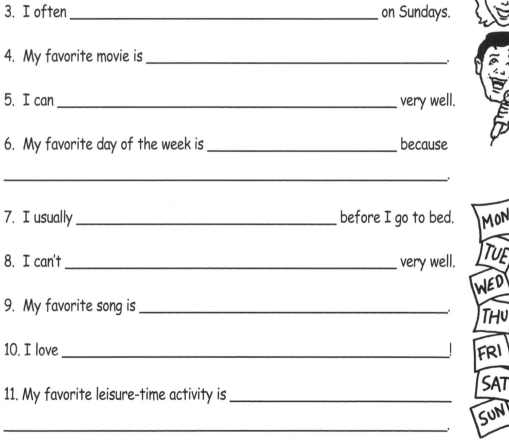

Job interview

Interaction
Whole class

Aim
To practice asking and answering questions about qualifications and abilities.

Time
15–20 minutes

Skills
Speaking

Grammar and functions
can / can't
Asking and answering questions about qualifications and abilities

Vocabulary
Review of words learned in unit 6

Preparation
Photocopy and cut apart the cards. Make sure there is one card for each student.

This game should be played with an even number of students. If there's an odd number of students in your class, have three students working together instead of two (two of the students form a team to partner a third one).

Make sure you have pairs of cards for students. If you have fewer than 20 students in your class, cut off boss and employee cards, as pairs, until you have one card for each student. If you have more than 20 students, repeat cards. Once again, make sure you have matching pairs of Boss and Employee cards for the students.

Answers

The cards are correctly matched on the worksheet.

Procedure

1   Prepare students for the activity by asking individual students questions like: *Do you work? What do you do? What do you do at work? What kind of programs do you use on your computer? Are you efficient / patient / friendly?*

2   Shuffle the cards and give them out, one to each student in class. Make sure that for every Boss card given, there's a corresponding Employee card.

3   Allow students one or two minutes to read the information on their cards. Check their understanding and answer any questions they may have.

4   Set the scene. Some of the students are bosses and some are employees. The bosses are looking for qualified people for a certain position. The employees are looking for a job.

5   Explain what the bosses and the employees have to do. The bosses should move around the room asking questions until they find someone who's qualified for the position. The employees should answer the bosses' questions and describe their abilities until they find the right job for their abilities and personalities.

6   Pretend you are a boss and model the activity, with a student role playing an employee. Use the first card on the worksheet as your example.

7   Set a time limit of ten minutes and ask students to start the activity. While the students are doing the activity, move around the room and give help if needed.

8   When the time is up, stop the activity.

9   Check whether bosses have found the employees they were looking for and whether the employees have found jobs.

Job interview

Boss	Employee
You're looking for a cook who can work at night, prepare French food and develop delivery spreadsheets on the computer.	You love food and you love cooking. You are a professional chef and take an online cooking course in your free time. You don't like waking up early because you stay up late at night trying new recipes.
You're looking for a bilingual teacher for kindergarten children.	You have three children and want to have three more. You speak Spanish and English and teach kindergarten at a local school.
You're looking for a sales manager who can travel all over the world. You want a person who speaks several languages and who understands Oriental culture.	You speak Japanese, Chinese, English and French. You always visit new cities on vacation and work as a sales manager for a multinational company in Japan.
You're looking for a trash collector to work at night. Your candidate doesn't need to have much education but needs to be in good physical shape and very strong.	You don't know what job you want. You don't speak a foreign language and you don't go to school. You work out in the gym every day and can run faster than all your friends. You enjoy working at night.
You're looking for a full-time secretary. You need a person who can type 60 words a minute and is good at using all programs on a computer.	You want a full-time job. You are a friendly, happy person and can type 90 words a minute. You love using computers and like working in offices.
You're looking for a full-time maid for your apartment. She needs to be a good cook and be able to clean well. You have two children and this person needs to take care of the children during the day.	You don't have much education but your house is always perfectly clean and your children are happy and get good grades in school. You can cook well and are looking for a full-time job during the day.
You're making a movie and need an action hero. This person needs to be handsome, strong, intelligent and a good actor. Experience as an actor is essential.	You are looking for a job in Hollywood. You have big muscles, you read three books a week and all the women love you. You make amateur movies with a friend in your free time.
You work at a new children's magazine and need a person to draw pictures for your next issue. Your ideal candidate draws well by hand and on the computer in a variety of styles. This person needs to draw quickly, too.	You go to art school and draw pictures all over your notebook during class. You draw well on the computer also. You work freelance for different kinds of magazines, including Marvel Comics and a magazine for golfers. You like short deadlines.
You need a part-time receptionist who is friendly, happy and efficient. Your ideal candidate needs to be able to answer the phone and make coffee.	You love to talk on the phone and you can only work part-time. You are happy, organized and friendly. You make great coffee!
You need a motorcycle delivery boy to take documents to customers. This person needs to own a motorcycle, ride it well and be familiar with the city.	You have a brand new motorcycle. You love riding it and you know your city well. You have a good map too. You are responsible and friendly.

Skyline Resource Pack 1. Published by Macmillan Publishers Limited.

I'm the President of the United States!

Interaction
Group work

Aim
To practice using the present simple with adverbs of frequency.

Time
15–20 minutes

Skills
Speaking
Listening

Grammar and functions
Adverbs of frequency
Present simple
Describing habits, interests and routines

Vocabulary
Action verbs

Preparation
Photocopy the worksheet, making sure there is one for each group of four students. Provide a dice and four pieces for each group.

Procedure

1 Prepare the students for the activity by telling them that you are a famous fashion model. Talk about yourself, using adverbs of frequency. Encourage students to ask you a few questions in the present simple such as *Where do you live?* or *What do you do in your free time?* Give imaginative answers to make it fun.

2 Ask students to pretend they are the President of the United States and invite them to talk about what they *usually, never, always* or *sometimes* do.

3 Ask students to form groups of four. Distribute the worksheets, dice and pieces.

4 Explain how to play the game.
   • Each player chooses a character from the bottom of the page or invents one of his / her own.
   • The players throw the dice and the player with the highest number goes first.
   • Each player throws the dice on his / her turn and moves his / her piece along the path.
   • Every time a player stops on a verb square, he / she has to make up a sentence, remembering who his / her character is. If other students think the sentence is "in character," the player can continue on his / her next turn. If he / she invents a sentence that is not "in character," he / she has to try again on the same square on his / her next turn.
   • Remind students that they need to use adverbs of frequency when making sentences.
   • There are rewards and penalties in this game. Rewards allow players to move ahead and penalties force them to go backwards or to miss a turn.
   • The player who reaches the last square (FINISH) first is the winner.

5 Ask students to start playing the game.

6 While students are playing, move around the classroom and give help if needed.

7 Stop the activity when the time is up.

Skyline Resource Pack 1. Published by Macmillan Publishers Limited.

I'm the President of the United States!

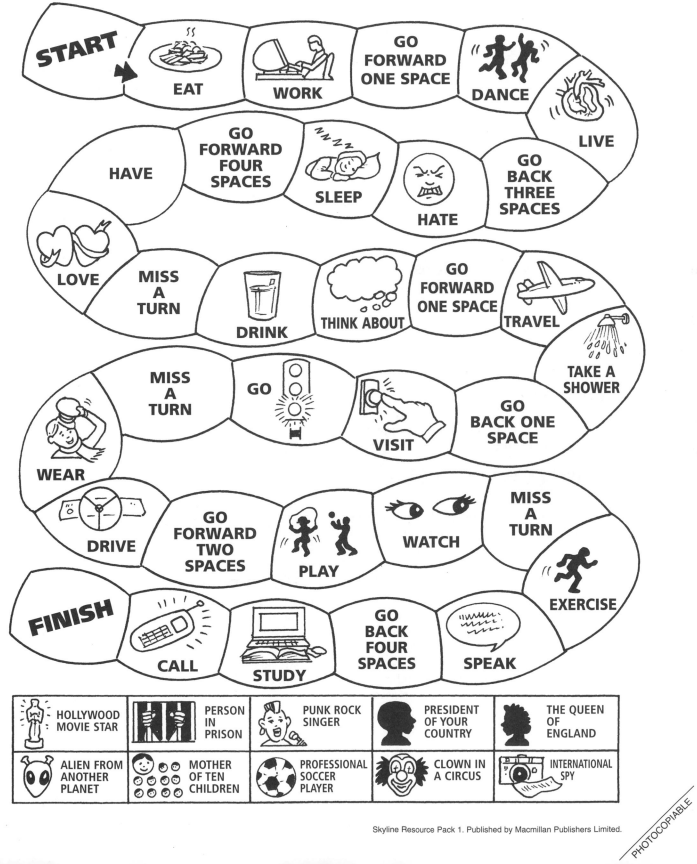

PHOTOCOPIABLE

What are they doing?

Interaction
Pair work

Aim
To practice asking and answering questions using the present progressive.

Time
15–20 minutes

Skills
Speaking
Listening

Grammar and functions
Questions and answers using the present progressive
Describing and comparing different activities

Vocabulary
Action verbs

Preparation
Photocopy and cut apart the A / B worksheets. Make enough copies for each pair of students to have an A and a B sheet.

Answers

Student A
Apt. 1C: The family is watching TV. Apt. 2C: The man / teenager is ironing his pants. Apt. 1B: The woman is eating ice cream and watching TV. Apt. 2B: The mother is holding her baby. Apt. 1A: The man is sleeping. Apt. 2A: The couple are kissing.
Student B
Apt. 1C: The family is playing a game. Apt. 2C: The man / teenager is vacuuming the rug. Apt. 1B: The woman is exercising. Apt. 2B: The father is holding his baby.
Apt. 1A: The man is drinking and watching TV.
Apt. 2A: The couple are leaving the apartment.

Procedure

1 Prepare students for the activity by asking individual students questions about where they live and what their neighbors are like, e.g. *Do you live in a house or in an apartment? Do you know your neighbors? Can you describe one of your neighbor's daily routines?*

2 Divide the students into two groups, A and B.

3 Distribute student A worksheets to group A and student B worksheets to group B.

4 Set the scene: Students A and B have similar pictures of an apartment building. They can see inside each of the apartments. They can see people doing different things.

5 Explain that students A and B should look at each apartment and talk about what they see happening. The objective of the game is to spot the differences.

6 Elicit the questions they might ask each other and write them on the board, e.g. *Look at Apartment 2A. How many people are there?* If necessary, play the part of a student A and model the activity with a student B.

7 Set a time limit of ten minutes and ask students to begin the activity.

8 Move about the classroom, checking if students are working correctly. Give help if needed.

9 When the time is up check students' answers.

Additional ideas
Give out the student A cards to group A and the student B cards to group B. Ask students to work in A / A and B / B pairs. One student chooses an apartment, e.g. *2A*. His / her partner has to guess the apartment he / she has chosen by asking *yes / no* questions, e.g. *Is there a man in your apartment? Is he ironing clothes?*

What are they doing?

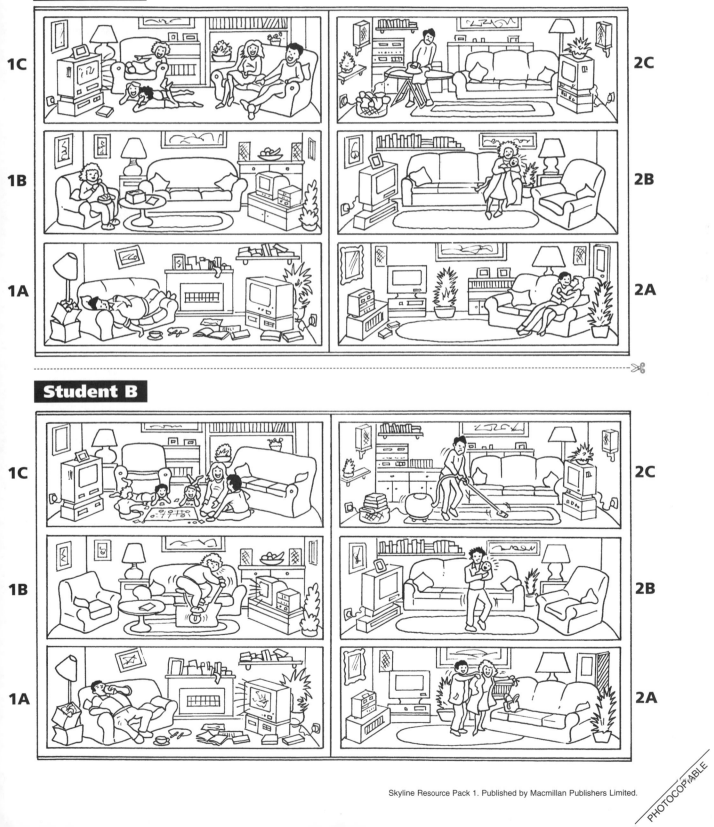

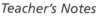

Are you jealous?

Interaction
Group work

Aim
To practice describing feelings and sharing opinions.

Time
15–20 minutes

Skills
Speaking
Listening

Grammar and functions
Present simple and present progressive
Describing feelings

Vocabulary
Adjectives to describe feelings

Preparation
Photocopy the worksheet. Make sure there's one for each student in the class.

Procedure

1 Prepare students for the activity by asking individual students questions, e.g. *Do you have a girlfriend / boyfriend? Is she / he a romantic person? What is she / he like?*

2 Give a worksheet to each student.

3 Allow students a few minutes to familiarize themselves with the information and answer any questions they might have.

4 Ask students to form groups of four.

5 Explain the task. Students should read the situations and choose a number from the scale that best describes their feelings. Remind students that they should discuss their answers with the group, but that the group doesn't have to agree on one answer. Each student should write down his / her own choice.

6 Set a time limit of ten minutes for this part of the activity. When the time is up, ask students to add up their scores.

7 Go through the scoresheet with the class. Make sure they understand it.

8 If time allows, talk to the students about their scores. Ask them if they agree / disagree with them. Encourage students to give reasons for their opinions and to discuss different situations from the quiz.

Option
Ask students to do this quiz in pairs, preferably with partners they know slightly. They read each question and predict how they think their partner will answer. Then they read the quiz together and check how accurate they were. If they don't know their partners well, they should do each prediction one by one.

Are you jealous?

Read the 12 situations below and choose a number from the scale that best describes your feelings. When you're finished, add up your scores.

Not at all upset 1	A little bit upset 2	Moderately upset 3	Very upset 4

_____ 1 You're at a fun party with your date. Your date is talking to an attractive person of the opposite sex and doesn't introduce you.

_____ 2 You ask your date out to dinner. He / she tells you he / she can't because he / she wants to stay home alone. You call that evening and no one answers the phone.

_____ 3 Your date isn't as romantic as before and likes watching TV more than spending time with you.

_____ 4 You and your date are at an office Christmas party. Your date receives several presents and one of them is very sexy.

_____ 5 You go to the gym every day but your date never does any exercise. One day, your date starts going to a different gym and seems very enthusiastic.

_____ 6 You're at a party and your date is getting a lot of attention from people of the opposite sex.

_____ 7 Your date takes a nap at your house and starts talking in his / her sleep. Over and over he / she says the name of someone you don't know.

_____ 8 You're at your date's house when the phone rings. You pick it up and the person on the other end hangs up immediately. This happens three times in one evening.

_____ 9 Your date has a very good friend of the opposite sex. He / she says there is no romantic interest between them and they're just friends but you feel they telephone and e-mail each other a lot.

_____ 10 Your date never asks you about your day-to-day life and isn't interested in your problems. When a friend comes over, he / she listens to the friend's problems with enthusiasm and support.

_____ 11 Your date wins the federal lottery but doesn't share any of the money with you.

_____ 12 Your date seems very interested in finding out all about your best friend.

Scoresheet

If you score from 12–20: You are not suspicious of your date. But do you really care about him / her?

If you score from 21–28: You are secure in your relationship and you trust your partner.

If you score from 29–38: You care very much about the relationship but maybe you're worried a bit too much?

If you score from 39–48: You spend a lot of time worrying about your relationship. A little jealousy can be healthy but too much can destroy your relationship.

What word is it?

Interaction
Team work

Aim
To practice defining words.

Time
15–20 minutes

Skills
Speaking
Listening

Grammar and functions
Recycling present simple and present progressive verbs
Defining words

Vocabulary
Review of words learned in units 1–7

Preparation
Photocopy and cut apart the 14 cue cards.

Procedure

1 Prepare students for the activity by telling them that you are going to define some words and that they have to tell you what words they are, e.g.
   Teacher: *It's a room in the house.*
   Students: *The kitchen?*
   Teacher: *No, there's a sofa there and you watch TV.*
   Students: *The living room!*

2 Divide the students into two teams (A and B).

3 Shuffle the cards and place them randomly on your table, face down.

4 Ask students in each group to choose a leader.

5 Leaders choose one of the cards on your table. Taking turns, one person from each team defines the words on the card, one by one, to their group. Students are not allowed to draw pictures or use gestures as part of their descriptions.

6 Give a point to the first team to complete a card. Allow 90 seconds as a maximum amount of time each team can take. Encourage them to hurry so their overall team score is better than their opponent's.

7 There are 14 different cards, so each team can play the game seven times.

9 The team with the highest score wins.

10 Make sure different students give the definitions each time.

Option
The game is played by two teams. Instead of defining all the words, leaders choose one of the words and mime or draw it on the board. Students guess the word.

Additional ideas
Write five categories on the board, e.g. a country, an adjective, a famous person, an animal, a verb. Students have one minute to write down one word from each category, on pieces of paper. Use their lists to play the game described above.

What word is it?

president inspector snow yellow computer	always traffic warm sumo wrestler lamp
honeymoon old noon practical sports	tour cold Friday migration fall
language restaurant Capricorn green elephant	aunt window garden Independence Day wind
violin stereo average cheap vegetable	nationality love hotel butterfly blond
sometimes painter name expensive bat	Asia party insect pollution winter
Las Vegas cloudy weekend Taurus modern	rain stressful grandmother university bathroom
Australia exercise furniture summer bed	spell Easter spring brown South America

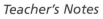

Is there a bank?

Interaction
Pair work

Aim
To practice asking and answering questions about places.
To practice reading a map.

Time
10–15 minutes

Skills
Speaking
Listening

Grammar and functions
Asking and answering questions about places
There is / there are
Prepositions of place

Vocabulary
Places around town

Preparation
Photocopy and cut apart the student A and student B cards. Make enough copies for each pair to have an A and a B card.

Procedure
1 Divide the students into two groups, A and B.

2 Give out the student A cards to group A and the student B cards to group B.

3 Explain what the students have to do. There are eight places on their maps which haven't been labeled. Their partners know where they are. Their task is to ask their partners questions and label the missing places on their maps.

4 Elicit the questions they might ask each other and write them on the board, e.g. *Is there a / an _____ on your map? Where is it?*

5 Play the part of a student A and model the activity with a student B.

6 Ask students to do the activity in A / B pairs.

7 Set a time limit of five minutes and ask the A students to start the activity.

8 When the time is up, ask students to change roles. This time, the B students start.

9 Allow them five minutes for this part of the activity.

10 When the time is up, ask students A and B to compare their maps.

Additional ideas
In groups of five, ask students to draw a map of an ideal district / street / neighborhood and then describe their map to the rest of the class. Students can do this individually also, drawing a map and then writing a short paragraph about it.

Is there a bank?

Student A

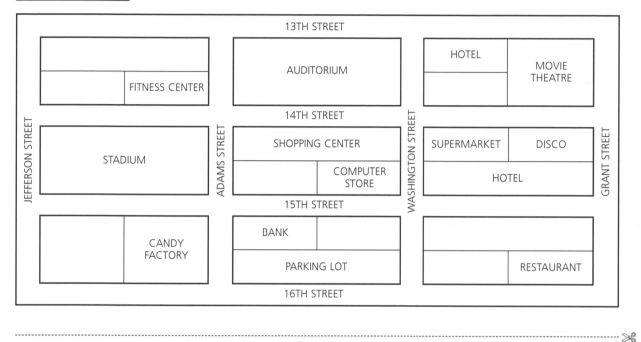

- ✂

Student B

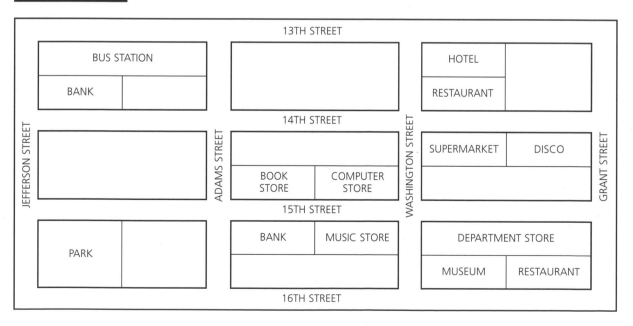

Cooperative crossword

Interaction
Pair work

Aim
To practice defining and describing places in the city.

Time
15–20 minutes

Skills
Speaking
Listening

Grammar and functions
Defining places around town

Vocabulary
Places around town

Preparation
Photocopy and cut apart the A / B cards. Make enough copies for each pair of students to have an A and a B card.

Answers

Procedure

1 Prepare the students for the activity by telling them you are going to describe a place in town and that they have to guess which place it is, e.g.
Teacher: We buy bread there.
Students: Bakery.

2 Divide the students into two groups, A and B.

3 Give the student A cards to group A and the student B cards to group B.

4 Explain that student A should help student B complete his / her puzzle by describing or defining the places that he / she has that student B doesn't have. Student B will do the same for student A.

5 Pre-teach the questions they might ask each other and write them on the board, e.g. *What's 1 across? What's 2 down?*

6 Remind students that they are not allowed to say the answers. They are only allowed to define the words.

7 Set a time limit of about ten minutes and ask students to complete the activity in A / B pairs.

8 When all pairs have finished, check their answers.

Additional ideas
In pairs or in groups of four or five, students prepare their own cooperative crossword puzzles. Write some categories on the board for the groups to choose from, e.g. countries, nationalities, occupations, numbers, colors, rooms or furniture.

Cooperative crossword

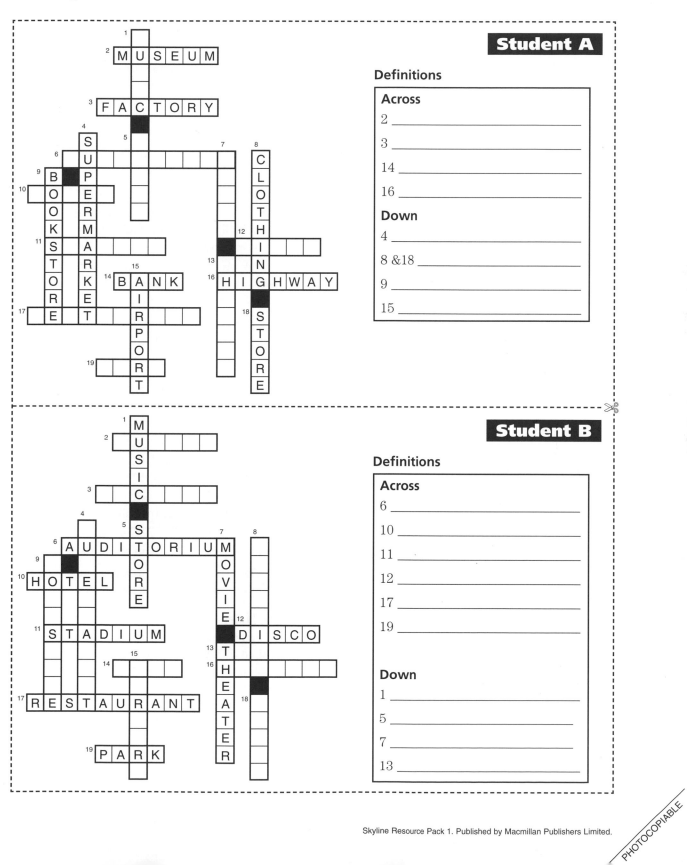

Student A

Definitions

Across

2 _____

3 _____

14 _____

16 _____

Down

4 _____

8 &18 _____

9 _____

15 _____

Student B

Definitions

Across

6 _____

10 _____

11 _____

12 _____

17 _____

19 _____

Down

1 _____

5 _____

7 _____

13 _____

They're getting married!

Interaction
Team work

Aim
To practice reading and understanding a sequence of events.

Time
15–20 minutes

Skills
Reading

Grammar and functions
The present progressive to express plans for the near future

Vocabulary
Words related to weddings

Preparation
Photocopy and cut apart the 20 sentences. Make sure you have one complete set for each team.

Answers
The sentences are in the correct order on the worksheet.

Procedure
1 Prepare the students for the activity. Introduce the topic by asking questions, e.g. *Are you single / married / about to get married? How do people prepare for a wedding ceremony in your country?*

2 While talking to the students, pre-teach new vocabulary and write the words on the board.

3 Divide the students into teams of twenty.

4 Set the scene. Jeanne and Max are getting married on Saturday night. There are lots of things they are going to do in the meantime.

5 Pick up a set of sentences, shuffle them and ask students from each team to choose one each and read it silently.

6 Allow them a few minutes to read their sentences and clarify any questions about vocabulary.

7 Explain what the teams have to do. Their objective is to reconstruct the story in the correct order. To do so, students have to read their sentences, one at a time and line up in the correct order.

8 Elicit the language they should use for the activity, e.g. *I think he's first. I think she's second.*

9 Set a time limit of ten minutes and ask students to start the activity.

10 Move around the room and give help if needed.

11 When time is up, ask teams to read their stories aloud to check the correct order.

Option
Ask students to work in groups of five. Give each student in the group four parts of the story. The group has to read the sentences and reconstruct the story.

Additional ideas
Ask students to write a paragraph about their plans for the next week, using the present progressive for future.

They're getting married!

On Friday morning, Max is getting his hair cut and having lunch with his mother.

After lunch, Max is picking up the rings downtown.

At 2 p.m., after he comes home from downtown, Max is taking a nap and then having a light dinner.

On Friday night, Max and his friends are having a stag party for his last night as a single man.

Max knows he's coming home from the party late so he's sleeping all day on Saturday.

On Saturday morning, Jeanne is getting a manicure and having lunch with some friends from college.

After lunch, Jeanne's returning to the beauty shop to get her hair and make-up done.

Jeanne's meeting her mother and bridesmaids at the church at 5 p.m. on Saturday afternoon to start getting dressed.

At 6 p.m., Max is coming to the church to start getting dressed for the ceremony.

The photographer is arriving at the church at 6:30 to start taking pictures of the guests arriving at the ceremony.

The preacher is arriving at 7:30 p.m.

Max's family is arriving at the church at 7:30 p.m. too.

The ceremony is starting at 8 p.m.

At 8:15 p.m., the happy couple are saying "I do" and Jeanne's mother is crying.

The wedding party is starting at 9 p.m.

Max and Jeanne are leaving at midnight on Saturday night for their honeymoon in Mexico.

They're taking a plane from Miami to Acapulco.

They're staying at a wonderful hotel called Hotel del Sol.

They're planning to take long walks on the beach and rest a lot at the hotel.

They're returning to the U.S. one week later.

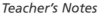

Mixed recipes

Interaction
Group work

Aim
To practice reading skills.

Skills
15–20 minutes

Time
Reading
Speaking

Grammar and functions
Imperatives

Vocabulary
Foods
Words related to cooking

Preparation
Photocopy and cut apart the recipe cards. Shuffle the cards, making sure you have one complete shuffled set for each group of four.

Answers

The recipes are in the correct order on the worksheet.

Procedure

1   Introduce the topic by asking questions, e.g. *Can you cook? Do you know how to fry an egg / make coffee? What's your favorite recipe?*

2   You may want to pre-teach the following words.
To beat – to mix something by stirring repeatedly.
Batter – a liquid mixture of flour, milk and eggs.
Yield – the amount produced.
Broth – a clear, thin soup.

3   Divide the students into groups of four. Give a set of recipe cards to each group.

4   Explain the task. The recipe cards are all mixed up. They have to read them, sort them out and reconstruct the two recipes.

5   Set a time limit of about ten minutes for the activity and ask groups to start the task.

6   The first group to come up with the two recipes in the correct order wins.

Option
Divide the class into two teams of at least 14. Give each team a set of shuffled cards and ask each student to take one card and read it silently. If there are more than 14 students in the team, let some work in pairs and share a card. At your signal, students within each team talk to each other to sort out the two recipes and put each of the recipes in the correct order. The first team to put both recipes in order correctly wins.

Additional ideas
Have students work in pairs or groups of four. Ask them to write the recipe for a traditional dish from their region or country.

Skyline Resource Pack 1. Published by Macmillan Publishers Limited.

Mixed recipes

The Best-Ever Brownies	Cream of Mushroom Soup
To begin, mix together in a large bowl: 2/3 cup flour 1/2 teaspoon baking powder 1/2 teaspoon salt 6 tablespoons cocoa powder	Begin by cooking 3/4 cup chopped onions in 1/4 cup butter. Cook five minutes.
In another bowl, mix together: 2 eggs 1 cup sugar 1/2 cup cooking oil 1 teaspoon vanilla	Add 2 cups chopped mushrooms to the onion mixture and cook, stirring, for another two minutes.
Add the flour mixture to the egg mixture and beat well.	Add 2 tablespoons flour to the mushrooms and onions and cook, stirring, for three minutes.
Pour batter into a greased pan.	Remove the fried mushrooms, onions and flour from the heat and add: 1 cup cream 1 cup vegetable broth
Bake in a medium oven for 15–20 minutes, but be sure to take it out when the batter is still sticky.	Bring the soup to a boil over low heat and cook gently for five minutes. Stir it the entire time.
When cool, cut and remove from pan.	Add salt and pepper and serve.
Yield: 20 brownies	Yield: 4 servings

Skyline Resource Pack 1. Published by Macmillan Publishers Limited.

Food race

Interaction
Pair work

Aim
To recycle vocabulary learned in unit 9.

Time
10–15 minutes

Skills
Speaking

Grammar and functions
Review of the present simple
Information and *yes / no* questions

Vocabulary
Different kinds of food
Food categories

Preparation
Photocopy the worksheet and cut apart the cards. Make sure you have one set for every pair of students in the class.

Answers

Fat, Oil and Sugar: chocolate cake, Coca-Cola, cookies, margarine
Milk, Yogurt and Cheese: parmesan cheese, chocolate milk, strawberry yogurt, mozzarella cheese
Proteins: peanuts, pork chops, lobster, roast beef, salmon, fried eggs, walnuts, soybeans, fried chicken
Vegetables: lettuce, vegetable soup, tomatoes, carrots, broccoli
Fruits: bananas, orange juice, apples, peaches, kiwi, apple juice
Bread, Cereal, Rice and Pasta: spaghetti, crackers, tortillas, rice, oatmeal, wholewheat bread, pita bread, cornflakes

Procedure
1   Ask students to form pairs.
2   Give each pair of students a set of cards.
3   Explain the task. They should sort the food cards into the appropriate categories. (See Answers for the categories.)
4   Allow students a few minutes to go through the food cards and check the vocabulary. Encourage them to use their dictionaries for kinds of food they don't immediately recognize.
5   Elicit the questions they might ask each other to sort the words, e.g. *Is strawberry yogurt a sugar or a milk product?* Write them on the board.
6   Set a time limit of eight minutes. Ask students to begin the activity.
7   Move around the room and give help if needed.
8   When the time is up, check students' answers. Say a category and ask different pairs to name kinds of food that go in that category. Some kinds of food, e.g. *strawberry yogurt,* can fit into two categories. Allow students to discuss their reasons for the answers they give, if they are different from yours.

Option
Photocopy and cut apart the food cards only. Make enough sets for every pair or small group. Ask students to form pairs or small groups. Write the headings Countable and Uncountable on the board and ask the pairs / groups to do the same on a piece of paper. Students sort out the food cards into the two categories.

Additional ideas
Ask students to work in pairs and use the food cards above, plus any additional words they might want to use, to make up three healthy meal plans. One should be for breakfast and the other two for lunch and dinner. After several minutes, ask students to share their plans with the rest of the class.

Food race

Fat, Oil and Sugar	Milk, Yogurt and Cheese	Proteins	Vegetables	Fruits	Bread, Cereal, Rice and Pasta

peanuts	Coca-Cola	pita bread
bananas	salmon	tomatoes
orange juice	parmesan cheese	apple juice
spaghetti	chocolate milk	walnuts
crackers	wholewheat bread	soybeans
pork chops	apples	cookies
tortillas	lettuce	mozzarella cheese
chocolate cake	peaches	margarine
lobster	strawberry yogurt	cornflakes
rice	vegetable soup	carrots
oatmeal	fried eggs	broccoli
roast beef	kiwi	fried chicken

Health quiz

Interaction
Group work

Aim
To practice talking about food, diets and lifestyles.

Time
15–20 minutes

Skills
Reading
Speaking

Grammar and functions
Frequency words
Information questions with the present simple

Vocabulary
Food
Eating habits
Leisure-time activities

Preparation
Photocopy the worksheet. Make sure there is one copy for each student.

Answers

Ask students to look at the answer key at the bottom of the worksheet and calculate their scores.

Procedure

1 Prepare the students for the activity. Introduce the topic by asking questions, e.g. *Do you consider yourself a healthy person? Do you smoke?*

2 Tell the students that they are going to take part in a quiz to see if they are healthy.

3 Ask students to form groups of four.

4 Give out the worksheets, one to each student.

5 Allow students a few minutes to read the questions and the multiple-choice alternatives. Answer any questions they may have about vocabulary.

6 Explain the activity. In groups, students read each of the questions and discuss their answers. Explain that they don't have to agree on a single answer, but rather talk about their habits with the group. They then mark their personal answer on their worksheet.

7 Allow them ten minutes to complete this part of the activity. Move around the room as they work and give help if needed.

8 Stop the activity when time is up and ask students to calculate their scores, using the key at the bottom of the worksheet.

9 When students have finished, allow them one or two minutes to read the comments at the bottom of the page. Then start a discussion on the comments themselves.

Option
Ask students to work in pairs. Student A reads the questions to student B and fills out the form for him / her. Student B shouldn't see the worksheet as this is happening. Student B does the same. Then students check their answers and discuss the results.

Additional ideas
Ask students to write ten sentences stating what they are going to do to be healthy or live a healthier lifestyle, e.g. *I'm going to eat my meals at home.*

Health quiz

Do the quiz below and find out if you're healthy!

1 How many glasses of water do you drink each day?
a One to two.
b Four to six.
c Eight to ten.

2 How often do you use sunscreen on your face and hands?
a Every day.
b Only when I'm on the beach or at the pool.
c Never.

3 How many servings of fruits and vegetables do you eat every day?
a One to two.
b Three to four.
c Five to eight.

4 How many hours do you sleep every night?
a Five to six.
b Seven to eight.
c Nine to ten.

5 Do you smoke?
a No, never.
b No, but those around me do.
c Yes, I do.

6 How often do you exercise?
a Once a month.
b Once a week.
c Three times a week.

7 How often do you feel stressed?
a Every day, all day.
b Once in a while and only in extremely stressful situations.
c Almost never.

8 What do you do when you feel stressed?
a I smoke a cigarette and get a cup of coffee.
b I breathe deeply, calmly express myself and, when possible, exercise a bit.
c I cry and shout.

9 How do you spend your free time?
a I try to catch up on all my pending work projects.
b I drink beer and watch TV.
c I visit friends and pursue my hobbies.

10 How many cups of coffee do you drink every day?
a Zero to one.
b Two to four.
c Five or more.

Count your answers:

1	c = 3 points; b = 2 points; a = 1 point
2	a = 3 points; b = 2 points; c = 1 point
3	c = 3 points; b = 2 points; a = 1 point
4	b = 3 points; c = 2 points; a = 1 point
5	a = 3 points; b = 2 points; c = 1 point
6	c = 3 points; b = 2 points; a = 1 point
7	c = 3 points; b = 2 points; a = 1 point
8	c = 3 points; b = 2 points; a = 1 point
9	c = 3 points; b = 2 points; a = 1 point
10	a = 3 points; b = 2 points; c = 1 point

Are you healthy?

24 to 30 points: You're doing really well! Keep up the healthy lifestyle and you'll live a long, happy life.

18 to 23 points: You need to think about your lifestyle. Get more excercise, more rest and work on your stress and you'll not only feel but you'll look better!

Under 17 points: Change your life now! You're in trouble – you're stressed, tired, out of shape and have some bad habits. It's time to think about what you're doing to yourself!

Question line up

Interaction
Whole class

Aim
To practice the present simple and past simple.

Time
15–20 minutes

Skills
Speaking
Listening

Grammar and functions
Review of major functions learned in previous units
Present simple and past simple in information questions and *yes / no* questions

Vocabulary
Review of words from units 1–10

Preparation
Photocopy and cut apart the 30 question cards. Make sure you have one question card for each student.

Procedure

1 Divide the students into two groups of equal number.

2 Call all the students from group A to come to the front of the class. Have them stand in a line facing the class.

3 Give each student in group A a card from the group A column.

4 Give them a minute to study their questions. Answer any questions they may have about their questions.

5 Ask the students from group B to stand in front of group A with one person from each group facing a person from the other group.

6 At your signal, every student from group A should ask his / her question to the student in front of him / her. When each pair has asked and answered that specific question, ask students in group B to move one person to the left. This will form a new pair and the students in group B will be asked new questions. The students in group A do not move.

7 Ask students to continue until all the students in group B have talked to all the students in group A.

8 Now ask group B to line up where group A was and give them their cue cards with questions. Repeat the process above.

9 Encourage students to answer the questions as honestly as possible. Encourage those asking the questions to really listen to the answers. One purpose of this exercise can be to get to know classmates better and increase rapport among the students.

Option
Divide the students into groups of five. Prepare various sets of question cards and make sure you have one complete set for each group. Give a set of cards to each group and ask students to randomly choose six question cards each. In turn, students question the other students in their groups.

Question line up

Group A	Group B
Where were you born?	Where did you go to high school?
Where would you like to travel on your next vacation?	Did you like math when you were younger?
What can you do really well?	Where did you go on vacation last year?
Did you travel abroad last year?	What star sign are you?
What did you do last Friday night?	What was your favorite TV show when you were a kid?
Are you single?	Did your family have a car when you were a kid?
Where did you go to primary school?	Do you usually do your homework?
What did you have for breakfast this morning?	What did you do last Saturday night?
Did you like English when you were younger?	Can you play a sport well? Which sport?
How did you come to class today / tonight?	What sports do you practice?
Do you like cooking?	What did you have for dinner last night?
Did you live in a house or an apartment when you were a kid?	How many people are there in your family?
Who was your favorite singer when you were a kid?	What time did you wake up this morning?
Where did you spend Christmas last year?	What would you like to eat for dinner tonight?
Do you often rent videos to watch at home?	Do you live alone?

Skyline Resource Pack 1. Published by Macmillan Publishers Limited.

Jumbled biographies

Interaction
Group work

Aim
To use the past simple to reconstruct biographies of famous musicians.

Time
15–20 minutes

Skills
Reading
Speaking
Listening

Grammar and functions
Past simple
Connectives

Vocabulary
Language used in biographies

Preparation
Photocopy, cut apart and shuffle the biography cards and pictures. Make sure you have one set of cards for each group of four students in the class.

Answers

The cards are in the correct order on the worksheet.

Procedure

1   Introduce the topic by asking some questions about John Lennon, Elvis Presley, Bob Marley and Christopher Wallace, e.g.
Who was _____? What nationality was he? What are some of the things he was famous for? Do you listen to his music?

2   Divide the students into groups of four.

3   Give a set of cards to each group. Ask students to take five cards each.

4   Allow students a few minutes to familiarize themselves with the information and vocabulary on their cards. Answer any questions about vocabulary which students may have. If possible, ask students to look up new words in a dictionary.

5   Explain the activity. Students have jumbled information about four different famous musicians. Their task is to sort out the cards and reconstruct the biographies in the correct order.

6   Set a time limit of ten minutes and ask students to begin.

7   When the time is up, check their answers.

8   As a possible follow-up activity, bring in the music of these musicians. Play parts of several songs and see if students can identify who it is.

Option
Divide the students into teams of twenty. Give each student on each team a card. Ask them to read their cards aloud and to form four lines, one for each biography. Students with picture cards should say the name of the person if they can.

Additional ideas
Ask students to form small groups. Tell them to decide on a famous person who is no longer living and write a short paragraph about this person. It can be a musician, actor / actress, politician, athlete or even a famous criminal.

Jumbled biographies

This famous rapper, whose real name was Christopher Wallace, was born in New York City and was a leader in the New York hip-hop scene.	This American singer, often called "The King" or "Elvis the Pelvis," started his career in 1956 with the rock and roll classic, *Heartbreak Hotel.*	This British musician was the founding member of the Beatles, a band which started its incredible career in Liverpool, England.	This legendary reggae musician was born in Nine Miles, Jamaica, in 1945 and recorded his first song, *Judge Not,* at age 16.
The New York rapper, also known as Biggie Smalls, worked as a drug dealer before he started making rap tapes in the basement of friends' houses.	In the late 1950s and 1960s, he appeared in numerous films such as *Bossa Nova Baby* and *Love Me Tender*, but he was famous for his singing, not his acting ability.	After the band broke up in 1970, he and his wife Yoko moved to the Dakota apartments in New York City. They worked together to promote world peace and recorded several albums.	He started a band, the Wailers, in 1963 and the Wailers' first song, *Simmer Down*, was an instant success in Jamaica.
In 1994, he entered the national scene with his million-selling album, *Ready to Die*. Although his lyrics focused on crime – robbing and killing – he won the Billboard Music Award of 1995 for best rap artist of the year.	He died in 1977, probably due to an overdose of prescription drugs. Fans from all over the world traveled to his Memphis, Tennessee home to pay tribute to the King.	One of the albums contains his most distinctive song, *Imagine*, recorded in 1971. His last album, *Double Fantasy,* was released in 1980.	After a long series of successful albums and concert tours, he received the United Nations' Peace Medal in 1978 for his attempt at reconciling two major Jamaican politicians, Prime Minister Manley and opposition leader Seaga.
In 1997, he was shot several times as he was sitting in his car after a party in Los Angeles. After his death, several leading rappers, including Snoop Doggy Dogg and Doug E. Fresh, attended a meeting in Chicago and agreed to a peace tour and an album.	After his death, his home, called Graceland, was opened to the public and is the second most visited home in the United States, after the White House in Washington D.C.	When coming home from a recording session with Yoko in 1980, he was shot five times by a fan, Mark Chapman, in front of his New York City apartment building. He died before reaching the hospital.	Even before the Peace Medal, doctors discovered melanoma cancer in his right foot. He died in Miami in 1981. His body was placed in a mausoleum in Nine Miles.

What do you know about Diana?

Interaction
Pair work

Aim
To practice asking and answering questions using the past simple.

Time
15–20 minutes

Skills
Speaking

Grammar and functions
Asking and answering questions about personal information
Past simple in information questions

Vocabulary
Words related to personal data

Preparation
Photocopy and cut apart the A / B cards. Make enough copies for each pair of students to have an A and a B card.

Answers

Full name: Lady Diana Spencer
Date of birth: July 1, 1961
Place of birth: Sandringham, England, United Kingdom
Sign: Cancer
Occupations: Former kindergarten teacher, Princess
Date of marriage: July 29, 1981
Place of marriage: St. Paul's Cathedral, London
Name of husband: Charles, Prince of Wales
Number of children: Two
Names of children: William and Harry
Date of divorce: July, 1996
Date of death: August 31, 1997
Place of death: Paris, France

Procedure

1 Introduce the topic. Ask students to tell you what they know about Diana Spencer. Ask questions, e.g. *Do you remember when Princess Diana died? How did she die? Why was she famous?*

2 Divide the students into two groups, A and B.

3 Give the A cards to the students in the A group and the B cards to the students in the B group.

4 Explain the activity. Each card contains some information about Princess Diana but it is incomplete. Ask students to complete the information on their cards by asking and answering with their partners.

5 Elicit the kind of questions they need to ask each other. If necessary, write the questions on the board for future reference.

6 Pretend you are student A and model the talk with a student B.

7 Set a time limit of about ten minutes and ask students to begin the task in A / B pairs.

8 When the time is up, ask students to compare their cards. They should check that they have given and received the correct information.

Additional ideas
Ask students to use the information on the cards (and other information they find in reference books or on the Internet) to write a short paragraph about Princess Diana.

What do you know about Diana?

Student A

Full name:	Lady Diana Spencer
Date of birth:	
Place of birth:	Sandringham, England, United Kingdom
Sign:	
Occupations:	Former kindergarten teacher, Princess
Date of marriage:	
Place of marriage:	St. Paul's Cathedral, London
Name of husband:	
Number of children:	Two
Names of children:	
Date of divorce:	July, 1996
Date of death:	
Place of death	Paris, France

✂

Student B

Full name:	
Date of birth:	July 1, 1961
Place of birth:	
Sign:	Cancer
Occupations:	
Date of marriage:	July 29, 1981
Place of marriage:	
Name of husband:	Charles, Prince of Wales
Number of children:	
Names of children:	William and Harry
Date of divorce:	
Date of death:	August 31, 1997
Place of death:	

How much do you know?

Interaction
Group work

Aim
To review the use of the past simple.

Time
10–15 minutes

Skills
Reading
Speaking

Grammar and functions
Past simple of regular and irregular verbs
Discussion of historical and cultural events

Vocabulary
Famous people

Preparation
Make photocopies of the worksheet. Make sure you have one copy for each student in the class.

Answers

1 b Leo Tolstoy
2 c Leonardo da Vinci
3 a Humphrey Bogart
4 c Ludwig van Beethoven
5 a Bruce Wayne
6 a Suicide
7 c George Washington
8 b Hamlet
9 a Austrian
10 c Bethlehem

Procedure

1 Tell students they are going to play a game to test their cultural literacy. Ask them a couple of questions, e.g. *Who was the last actor to play James Bond?* (Pierce Brosnan) *When did the U.S. declare its independence?* (1776)

2 Divide the students into groups of four or five.

3 Give a copy of the worksheet to each student.

4 Explain that groups of students should talk among themselves and check the right answers to the questions on the worksheet.

5 Set a time limit of ten minutes. Ask students to start the activity.

6 When the time is up, check students' answers.

7 Give 10 points for every correct answer and make notes of each group's score on the board.

8 The team with the highest score wins.

Option
Divide the students into two teams, A and B. Read the first question without the multiple-choice answers. The first student to raise his / her hand is allowed to answer the question for his / her team. If the answer is not correct, the other team is then allowed to answer. If neither team can answer a question, give them the three multiple-choice options as a means of helping them out. Give 10 points for every correct answer. The team with the highest score wins.

Additional ideas
In teams, students write up ten trivia questions similar to those on the worksheet. Team A then questions team B and vice versa. The team with most correct answers wins.

How much do you know?

Questions	Answers
1 Who wrote War and Peace?	a Fedor Mikhailovich Dostoievsky b Leo Tolstoy c Mikhail Gorbachov
2 Who painted the Mona Lisa?	a Michelangelo Buonarroti b Benito Mussolini c Leonardo da Vinci
3 Who starred in Casablanca?	a Humphrey Bogart b Clark Gable c Tom Cruise
4 Who wrote Beethoven's Ninth Symphony?	a J. S. Bach b George F. Handel c Ludwig van Beethoven
5 What was Batman's real name?	a Bruce Wayne b Barbara Gordon c Clark Kent
6 How did Vincent Van Gogh die?	a Suicide b Car accident c Plane accident
7 Who was the first president of the United States?	a John F. Kennedy b Franklin D. Roosevelt c George Washington
8 Who said, "To be or not to be? That is the question."?	a Pelé b Hamlet c Hitler
9 What nationality was Wolfgang Amadeus Mozart?	a Austrian b German c British
10 Where was Jesus Christ born?	a Jerusalem b Nazareth c Bethlehem

Once upon a time ...

Interaction
Whole class

Aim
To practice describing a sequence of events in the past.

Time
15–20 minutes

Skills
Speaking
Listening

Grammar and functions
Past simple
Connectives

Vocabulary
Review of words from units 1–11

Preparation
Photocopy and cut apart the verb cards. Make sure you have one card for each student in the class. If you have more than 38 students, make an extra copy of the worksheet and give repeat cards to the additional students.

Procedure

1 Introduce the topic by asking the students if they remember some of the stories they were told by their mothers when they were young. Choose one of those stories, e.g. *Little Red Hiding Hood.* Ask students if they remember the whole story.

2 Start telling that story and invite individual students to continue, e.g.
   Teacher: *Once upon a time, a little girl was walking along in the forest. She was carrying a basket of food for her grandmother.*
   Student A: *There was a wolf in the forest, waiting for her.*
   Student B: *He wanted to eat Little Red Riding Hood.*
   Continue like this until students understand the concept of creating a story, one sentence at a time.

3 Give each student a cue card and explain the activity. You are going to start telling a story and each student will add one or two sentences to it. Remind them that their sentences should include the verb on their card and that the story should be told in the past tense.

4 Start telling a story by saying *Once upon a time there was a* ____. (Insert an interesting noun here.) Have a student continue the story. This student should use the past tense form of the verb on his / her card to make the sentence. The story you create as a class can be absurd, it doesn't have to follow a known fairytale storyline. If the student you call on can't think of a semi-appropriate sentence, ask another student to contribute.

5 Continue creating a story until all students have contributed.

Additional ideas
Ask students to form groups of four. Distribute cards and ask groups to write a mini-story with four to eight of the cards they've been given.

Skyline Resource Pack 1. Published by Macmillan Publishers Limited.

Once upon a time ...

see	burn
wear	hope
kill	divorce
hear	eat
watch	begin
like	help
prepare	push
vomit	appear
drink	cook
need	fly
capture	sleep
jump	come
love	get married
run	answer
dance	speak
hit	carry
go	fall
escape	hate
want	open

What did you have for dinner last night?

Interaction
Group work

Aim
To practice using the past simple in *yes / no* questions and information questions.

Time
15–20 minutes

Skills
Speaking
Reading
Listening

Grammar and functions
Past simple

Vocabulary
Review of words from units 1–11

Preparation
Photocopy the worksheet. Make sure you have one for each group of four students. Provide a dice and four pieces for each group.

Procedure
1   Ask students to form groups of four.
2   Give out the worksheets, one to each group of students.
3   Give each group a dice and four pieces.
4   Explain how to play the game.
    • Taking turns, students throw the dice. The student with the highest number goes first.
    • Students throw the dice and move their pieces along the line. If a player stops on a square with a question, he / she has to read it aloud and answer it.
    • The other students then decide if the answer is acceptable or not. If it is, the student may stay on that square. If his / her answer is not accepted by the group, he / she must return to where he / she was and roll again on the next turn.
    • There are rewards and penalties in this game. Rewards allow players to move ahead, and penalties force them to go backwards or lose a turn.
    • The student who reaches the FINISH square first is the winner.
5   Set a time limit of about fifteen minutes and ask students to start playing the game.
6   Tell students that if they are not sure whether an answer is correct or not, they should ask for your help.

What did you have for dinner last night?

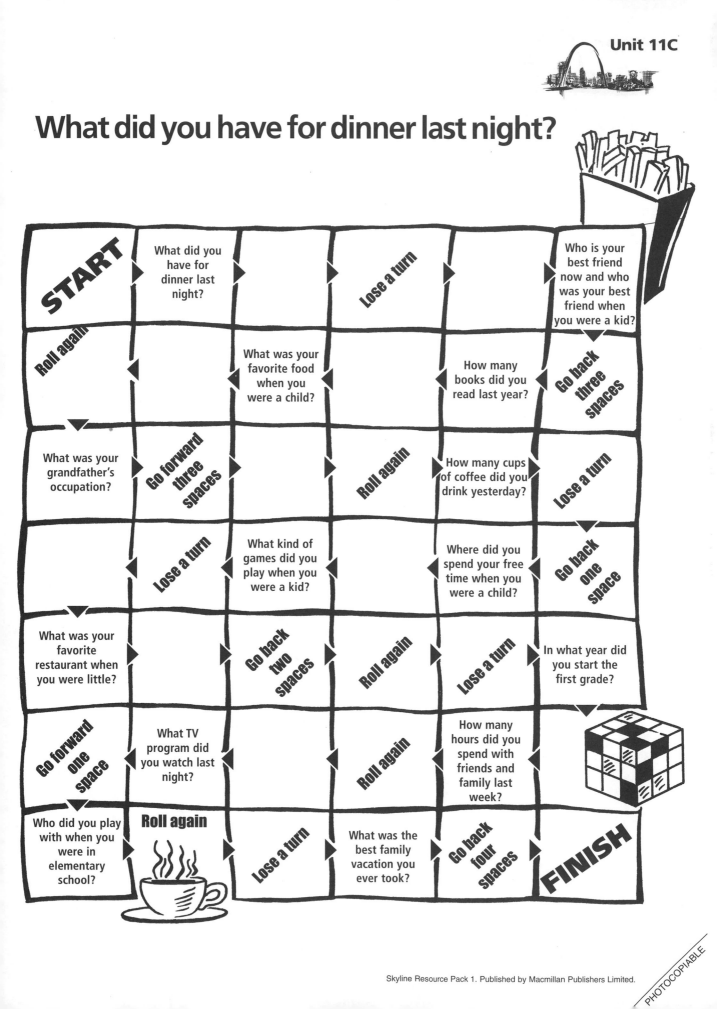

What's Jennifer going to do?

Interaction
Pair work

Aim
To practice using the future with *going to*.

Time
10–15 minutes

Skills
Speaking
Listening

Grammar and functions
Future with *going to*
Talking about future arrangements and plans

Vocabulary
Days of the week
Clock times
Action verbs

Preparation
Photocopy and cut apart the A / B cards. Make enough copies for each pair of students to have an A and a B card.

Procedure

1   Introduce the topic by asking the students questions, e.g. *Are you going to eat out after class? What are you going to do tomorrow morning? What are you going to do on your vacation?*
    Encourage different students to think of *going to* questions to ask their classmates.

2   Divide the students into two teams, A and B.

3   Give the student A cards to team A and the student B cards to team B.

4   Set the scene. They have a page of Jennifer's datebook but there are some notes missing.

5   Explain the activity. In pairs, students should talk to each other and complete Jennifer's datebook.

6   Elicit the questions students might ask each other and write them on the board, e.g. *What is Jennifer going to do at 10:00 a.m. on Sunday? What time is she going to go to bed on Monday?*

7   Set a time limit of about ten minutes and ask students to begin the activity in A / B pairs.

8   When the time is up, ask pairs to compare their cards and check their answers.

Additional ideas
Ask students to interview their partners about their plans for the coming week. They should make a small table like Jennifer's datebook and elicit as many details as they can. They should then write a short paragraph about their partner's plans.

What's Jennifer going to do?

Sunday, September 14

8:00	
9:00	
10:00	(Until 11:30) Brunch with Max Leone – talk about next movie, Flying Cowboys
11:00	
12:00	Workout at gym + shower, coffee with Barbara Streirock
1:00	
2:00	
3:00	
4:00	Nap
5:00	
6:00	
7:00	Dinner at Café Scapetti
8:00	(Until ??) Party at Tina Crumwell's penthouse
9:00	

Monday, September 15

8:00	Water aerobics
9:00	
10:00	Meeting at Universal Studios – talk about new video package with Steve Beam
11:00	
12:00	Lunch at Tino's Restaurant with Nancy Pillsbury – talk about Flying Cowboys hairstyle
1:00	
2:00	
3:00	
4:00	
5:00	Dentist appointment with Dr. Brenner
6:00	
7:00	Dinner with Marshall Winn – talk about Rats in the Attic CD-Rom
8:00	
9:00	

Sunday, September 14

8:00	
9:00	Wake up
10:00	
11:00	
12:00	
1:00	Lunch with Pete – talk about new CD with Marco Filetto
2:00	(Until 3:45) Attend inauguration of new salon with Jake
3:00	
4:00	
5:00	Do make-up, nails and hair at Freddo's
6:00	Cocktails with Flying Cowboys cast
7:00	
8:00	
9:00	

Monday, September 15

8:00	
9:00	Breakfast with Sid Nero
10:00	
11:00	(Until 11:45) Shopping on Rodeo Drive
12:00	
1:00	
2:00	(Until 3:30) Rehearsal for Flying Cowboys
3:00	
4:00	Nap
5:00	
6:00	(Until 6:45) Happy hour with Luke Bridgewater
7:00	
8:00	
9:00	In bed!

What should I do?

Interaction
Whole class

Aim
To practice using the modal auxiliary *should*.

Time
15–20 minutes

Skills
Speaking
Reading

Grammar and functions
Modal auxiliary *should*
Describing a problem
Asking for and giving advice

Vocabulary
Review of words learned in unit 12

Preparation
Photocopy and cut apart the cards. Make sure you have one card for each student in the class and that for each problem card there's a corresponding advice card. If you have less than twenty students in the class, take out some cards, making sure to remove corresponding pairs. If you have more than twenty students in the class, duplicate some of the pairs.
Note: This activity should be played by an even number of students. If there's an odd number of students in the class, one student should pair up with another student and work as a pair using one card.

Answers

The cards are in the correct order on the worksheet.

Procedure

1   Introduce the topic by describing a problem and asking students for advice, e.g. *My husband / wife thinks I spend too much money. What should I do?*

2   When you are sure students are comfortable with the use of the modal auxiliary *should*, shuffle the cards and distribute them randomly, giving one to each student in the class.

3   Explain the activity. Some students have problem cards and others have advice cards. The students with the problem cards should move around the room asking for advice. The students with the advice cards should move around the room giving advice to students with problems.

4   The object of the game is to find matching pairs.

5   Allow students some minutes to read their cards and familiarize themselves with the information.

6   Set a time limit of ten minutes and ask them to start the activity.

7   When students find their partners, ask them to go to the front of the class and stay together.

8   When time is up, ask each pair to read its problem and advice aloud. Check that there's a suitable piece of advice for each problem.

Option
Give a problem or advice card to each student in the class. Tell the students with the problem cards to write down a suitable piece of advice for that problem. Tell the students with the advice cards to think up a problem to match the piece of advice they have received.

Additional ideas
Divide the students into three groups. Write three complicated problems on the board and ask each group of students to choose one to discuss, e.g. *You find out your best friend is a drug dealer. What should you do?*

What should I do?

Problem Cards	Advice cards
You are exercising with your best friend when she stops running and says her chest hurts.	You should take her to a cardiologist.
You are spending too much money on paper for your printer.	You should try to recycle paper and use both sides when you print documents.
You eat too much ice cream and chocolate and can't fit into your jeans.	You should try to eat more fruit and vegetables.
You want to travel to Florida for Christmas but you don't have enough money right now.	You should try to get a temporary job to earn a little more money before December.
You are at a party when you see a very attractive person you don't know.	You should go talk to that person and see if he / she wants to go out on a date.
Your car has been broken into three times in the past month.	You should buy a car alarm and park in a safer place.
Your boss gave you a big project to do in one week but you won't have time to finish it.	You should try to get an assistant to help you.
A person you don't like very much is worried that he / she is going to fail the English test tomorrow.	You should offer to help this person study for the test.
Your aunt was in a car accident and is in the hospital.	You should buy some flowers and visit her to cheer her up.
Your sister is going to marry a man who doesn't love her.	You should try to stop her from getting married.

Life's big moments

Interaction
Whole class

Aim
To recycle the present simple, past simple and future with *going to*.
To review the modal auxiliary *should*.

Time
20–25 minutes

Skills
Reading
Writing
Speaking

Grammar and functions
Present simple, past simple, future with *going to*
Should
Giving opinions and justifying them

Vocabulary
Life events
Experiences
Plans

Preparation
Photocopy the worksheet. Make sure you have one copy for each student.

Procedure
1   Give out the worksheets, one to each student.

2   Ask students to complete the sentences with information about themselves. Remind them not to write their names on the sheet.

3   Allow students ten minutes to fill out the forms. When the time is up, collect the worksheets.

4   Shuffle the worksheets and give them out again, one to each student in the class. Take care not to give a student his / her own sheet.

5   Explain the activity. Students should read the information on the worksheet they have been given and move around the room, asking questions. Their objective is to find the person who wrote it.

6   Set a time limit of ten minutes for this part of the activity. When the time is up, check to see that students have found the correct person. Those that haven't found their partners should now read a few answers aloud and ask the person who wrote them to raise his / her hand.

Option
Ask students to work in pairs, interviewing their partners and writing their answers on their worksheets. They should then talk about their partners in front of the class, giving interesting details about their partners.

Additional ideas
Ask students to write a short paragraph about themselves or the person whose worksheet they were given.

Life's big moments

1 The most important year in my life was _____ because _____
_____
_____.

2 I have three objectives for next year.
I'm going to _____.
I'm going to _____.
I'm going to _____.

3 As a kid, the most important person in my life was _____
because _____
_____
_____.

4 The most important person in my life now is _____ because
_____
_____.

5 I think the most important thing to remember in life is _____
_____.

6 I think my family and friends should _____
_____
_____.

Macmillan Education
Between Towns Road, Oxford OX4 3PP
A division of Macmillan Publishers Limited
Companies and representatives throughout the world

ISBN-13 : 978 0 333 92659 8

First published 2001

Designed and illustrated by Red Giraffe

Cover photograph by Stone

Printed in Thailand

2011   2010   2009   2008   2007
10   9   8   7   6   7   6   5   4   3